Danube Bike Trail 3

From Vienna to Budapest

An original *cycline* guide

Esterbauer

cycline® Danube Bike Trail 3
© 2006, **Verlag Esterbauer GmbH**
A-3751 Rodingersdorf, Hauptstr. 31
Tel.: ++43/2983/28982, Fax: -500
E-Mail: bikeline@esterbauer.com
www.esterbauer.com

1st edition 2006
ISBN-10: 3-85000-212-8
ISBN-13: 978-3-85000-212-7

We wish to thank all the people who contributed to the production of this book.
The *cycline*-Team: Birgit Albrecht, Heidi Authried, Beatrix Bauer, Grischa Begaß, Karin Brunner, Anita Daffert, Nadine Dittmann, Stefan Dörner-Schmelz, Sandra Eisner, Roland Esterbauer, Angela Frischauf, Jutta Gröschel, Dagmar Güldenpfennig, Carmen Hager, Karl Heinzel, Heidi Huber, Peter Knaus, Martina Kreindl, Veronika Loidolt, Niki Nowak, Maria Pfaunz, Andreas Prinz, Adele Pichl, Petra Riss, Gaby Sipöcz, Martha Siegl, Matthias Thal, Wolfgang Zangerl.
Photo credits: Roland Esterbauer: Cover, 21, 22, 36, 40, 52, 60, 61, 62, 66, 82, 84, 86, 90, 92, 94, 101, 102,103, 104, 105, 107, 108, 110, 112, 114, 116; Birgit Albrecht: 8; Wiener Tourismusverband: 18; Marktgemeinde Orth: 28; Archiv: 32; Hungarian tourism office: 44, 48, 56, 68, 76; Bernhard Mues: 58, 100; Tourinform Györ: 64

Preface

The Danube Bicycle Route from Vienna to Budapest is the logical extension of the most popular cycling route in Europe, the Danube Bicycle Route from Passau to Vienna. A little wilder, but just as interesting, the 340-kilometer ride passes through parts of Austria, Slovakia and Hungary. The cycling tourist can look forward to excellent cycling paths on the dikes that line the Danube in Austria and Slovakia, quiet country roads, pristine villages, and culturally interesting cities like Györ, Tata and Esztergom in Hungary, the Danube's scenic "knee" north of Budapest, and of course the ancient and exquisite Hungarian capital city itself.

This bicycle touring atlas includes detailed maps of the countryside and of many cities and towns, precise route descriptions, information about historic and cultural sites as well as background information and a comprehensive list of overnight accommodations. The one thing this atlas cannot provide is fine cycling weather, but we hope you encounter nothing but sunshine and gentle tailwinds.

Map legend

The following colour coding is used:

———————— main cycle route

———————— cycle path / main cycle route without motor traffic

———————— excursion or alternative route

- - - - - - planned cycle path

The surface is indicated by broken lines:

———————— paved road

— — — — unpaved road

- - ▪ - ▪ - bad surface

Routes with motor traffic are indicated by dotted lines:

• • • • • • • cycle route with moderate motor traffic

• • • • • • • cycle route with heavy motor traffic

• • • • • • • cycle lane

road with heavy motor traffic

→ steep gradient, uphill

→ light gradient

⌐3⌐ distance in km

➤ cycle route direction

Scale 1 : 75. 000

1 cm = 750 m   1 km ≙ 13,3 mm

<u>City</u> picturesque town

( ) facilities available

🛏 🏠 hotel, guesthouse; youth hostel

🅰 ⛺ camping site; simple tent site

ℹ 🛒 tourist information; shopping facilities

🍴 🛋 restaurant; resting place*

🏊 🏊 outdoor swimming pool; indoor swimming pool

🔵 🔵 🔵 buildings of interest

✳ **Mill** other place of interest

🏛 🎭 🔱 museum; theatre; excavation

🦁 🌲 zoo; nature reserve

❋ ❋ panoramic view

—🚢— ferry

🔧 🚲 bike workshop; bike rental

🚲 🚲 covered ~; lockable bike stands

* selection

⛪ church; chapel; monastery

🏰 castle; ruins

🗼 tower; TV/radio tower

⚡ power station; transformer

�windmill; windturbine

✝ wayside cross; peak

⛏ mine; lighthouse

◯🏛 sports field; monument

✈ airport, airfield

⚓ boat landing

♀ natural spring; waste water

∽ treatment plant

⚠ ⚠ dangerous section; read text carefully

◣)(stairs; narrow pass, bottleneck

X X X road closed to cyclists

in city maps:

🅿 🅿 parking lot; garage

✉ 🅰 🅷 post office; pharmacy; hospital

🄵 🅄 fire-brigade; police

---

0 1 2 3 4 5 6 7 8 9 10 11 12 13 14 15

international border	
border checkpoint	
country border	
forest	
rock, cliff	
marshy ground	
vineyard	
cemetary	
shallows	
dunes	
meadows	
embankment, dyke	
dam, groyne, breakwater	
motorway	
main road	
minor road	
carriageway	
footpath	
road under construction	
railway with station	
narrow gage railway	
tunnel; bridge	

Contents

5

The Danube Bike Trail – Vienna to Budapest

The Blue Danube by Johann Strauss has forever linked the Danube's flow with the waltz's three-quarters time. When Strauss wrote the piece, the Danube's waters were already dark, as dark as the Austrians' mood following their defeat against the Prussians at Königsgrätz in 1866.

It was also during that period that the Austrian capital decided to attempt to control the river's flow to put an end to the floods that frequently caused great damage. The project was completed in 1875, and since then the stream that flows through the old city is known as the Danube canal.

Downstream from Vienna, the river is lined by deep and lush flood plains, at the edge of which generations of Austrian monarchs built their comfortable summer residences.

Near the right bank of the Danube one can find the traces of Carnuntum, one of the Roman Empire's most important cities. Its ruins lie beyond several side-arms of the river, away from the main stream. The last larger settlement on the Austrian side of the river is the town of Hainburg, from where the imperial tobacco company's vessels once set forth with their valuable freight. At the confluence of the Danube and the March stand the ruins of the ancient Theben fortress, and in the distance the castle in Bratislava can be seen. A border stone near here marks the end of the western world, but the Danube ignores such categories and merely changes its name: to "Dunav" in Slovakian and "Duna" in Hungarian. The stretch of the river between Hainburg and Bratislava is often called the "Hungarian Gate," where the Danube breaks through the Hainburg mountains on one side and the Small Carpathians on the other and enters the Small Hungarian Plain, where it forms the border between Slovakia and Hungary.

At the eastern end of the Small Hungarian Plain before the river runs into another range of mountains, there appears in the distance a great dome like some optical illusion that blocks light and the river's flow. It is the Esztergom Cathedral, modeled after St. Peters Cathedral in Rome, and seat of the Hungarian Roman Catholic primate. The classical basilica forms one of the three monumental Hungarian edifices that line the Danube. The other two are the Parliament in Pest and the castle in Buda.

Downstream from Esztergom the Danube continues towards the east before the river narrows between Zebegény and Visegrád. The river's flow accelerates, forming dangerous eddies and currents, before it slows again as it passes through Visegrád. The Danube then curves around tall boulders, breaks through the mountains and turns toward the old city of Vác.

On the right bank, the river flows past the beautiful small town of Szentendre, which still looks much unchanged from how it was built in the 18th century. Szentendre's narrow streets, its many church towers, the wooden staircases, steep alleys, covered walkways and gardens create an inviting atmosphere for romantic walks. The town has a significant Serbian community, which gives it a southerly flair mixed with the smell of garlic from hot "lángos," the delicious Hungarian fried bread.

Just beyond Szentendre lies Budapest. From the Danube's source in the Black Forest to its mouth on the Black Sea, there is no other place where the graceful river is enclosed with greater magnificence, generosity and dignity than in the Hungarian capital. This is where the Danube finds its "golden section" with a city that greets visitors with light and life.

The Route

Length

The total length of the Danube Bike Trail from Vienna to Budapest is 299 or 306 kilometers on the Slovak side of the river, and 346 or 353 kilometers on the Hungarian side. This does not include side trips and alternative route possibilities.

Surface quality and traffic

The road quality on the Danube bicycle route from Vienna to Budapest varies greatly according to region and country. In Austria, all but a very short section is well developed, mostly following a paved path without motorized traffic on the Hubertusdamm.

Completion of the major hydro-electric plant on the Danube in Slovakia has also resulted in outstanding paved bicycle paths on the crowns of the dikes on both sides of the river. On the left side, this road is interrupted, but on the right side it goes all the way to Medved'ov. For this reason, only the route on the right side is described in these pages. Between Medved'ov and Štúrovo the route alternates between public roads and paths along the river, some of which are not paved.

Hungary has undertaken significant improvements. The Danube bicycle route is posted and stays close to the river. A bicycle path has been completed from Ásványráro to just behind Györ. From Bönyrétalap to Bábolna the route uses a more heavily-traveled road.

To Táta the route follows the main national

road at times, or hilly but quieter country lanes. Another section of bicycle path begins in Esztergom, but is followed by a few kilometers with traffic. After the ferry to Szob it is possible to ride along the left bank of the river. Near Vác the route goes onto Szentendre Island before crossing to the right bank and the town of Szentendre. On the right bank, the route mostly runs on public roads with traffic. Downstream from Szentendre the Danube bicycle route is posted with signs along the right bank of the river.

Signage

Posted signs marking the route also vary from country to country. In Austria, the Danube bicycle route is posted uniformly with large green rectangular signs. Slovakia uses the same signs on both sides of the dam, as far as Medved'ov. Hungary has marked the Danube bicycle route with different green signs, but these are not to be found along the entire route. From Ásványráró to Györ,

Bicycle route sign near Medved'ov

from Zebegény to Göd and from Szentendre to Budapest. All bicycle trails and routes in Budapest are marked.

Important telephone numbers

International telephone codes:

Hungary: 0036
Slovakia: 00421
Austria: 0043

Hungarian tourism offices:
in Vienna: ☎ 01/5852012
in Frankfurt: ☎ 069/9291190

Danube bicycle route sign in Hungary

Information

Additional information is available from regional tourism offices:

Tourist Information Vienna, Albertinerplatz, 1010 Vienna, ☎ 01/24555
E-Mail: wienhotels@wien.info
www.info.wien.at
Slovakian tourist office in

Austria, Fillgradergasse 7/4, 1060 Wien, ☎ (0)1/5139569
Slovak Tourist Board, SK-85005 Bratislava, Bajkalska 25/a, ☎ 7/48245023-4
Bratislava Information Service, SK-81428 Bratislava Klobčnicka 2, ☎ 2/54433715
Hungarian tourist office Vienna, Opernring 5/2, A-1010 Wien, ☎ (0)1/585201210,
Info-Telephone Hungary, ☎ 00800/36000000 (free of charge)
Hungarian tourist office, H-1024 Budapest, Steindl Imre utca 12, ☎ (0)1/3532956, oder 1/4280377
Association of Hungarian Travelling Bicyclists, H-1065 Budapest, Pf. 483, ☎ (0)1/331-2467
KEROSZ Hungarian Bicycle Association, H-1119 Budapest, Hadak útja. 64/A, ☎ (0)1/206-6223
VBB Association of the friends of City Cyclists, H-1053 Budapest, Curia u. 3. II/1, ☎ (0)1/309227064

Arrival & departure

Both Vienna, the starting point of this tour, and the destination, Budapest, offer extensive international travel connections by rail and air. The international airport at Frankfurt/Main is, after London´s Heathrow, the second-largest airport in Europe and offers excellent connections to international routes.

Once you have arrived in Europe, trains and buses offer excellent alternatives to air travel. Trains provide comfortable second class wagons though the traveller should be aware that train fares have become significantly more expensive in recent years. When purchasing tickets always ask what discounts are available. Young travellers can take advantage of special fares, and tickets are usually cheaper if they are ordered in advance. Bus lines offer lower prices, but are usually less comfortable and take longer.

It always makes sense to carefully compare the costs of travelling by train, airplane or bus.

By rail

Information:
ÖBB (Austrian Rail): ☎ 01/51717, www.oebb.at
MÁV, Hungarian Rail, domestic information ☎ 1/461-5400, international information ☎ 1/461-5500
FÖVINFORM, road traffic information, ☎ 1/17-1173
ZSR, Slovakian Rail, Bratislava, ☎ 02/50581111
Vienna is relatively easy to reach by rail. General regulations regarding the transport of bicycles on Austrian trains are described below.

For the return trip from Budapest, plan to spend several hours at the train station obtaining information, tickets and reservations. Especially in the main season, trains and train stations tend to be crowded and railroad personnel overworked.

Information, Keleti pu:

Budapest, ☎ 1/327866.
Some of the main international trains that can accommodate bicycles in the summer months are listed here:

Budapest-Keleti pu.
6:05 o'clock (739/346)
Wien Westbahnhof
(Vienna West-train station)   9:04 o'clock
Budapest-Keleti pu.   15:50 o'clock(IC 793/344)
Wien Westbahnhof   18:40 o'clock
Budapest-Keleti pu.   20:25 o'clock (EN 268)
Wien Westbahnhof   23:15 o'clock-23:25 o'clock
As an alternative, you may consider taking a ship up the river from Budapest to Vienna.

More information about this option can be found in the Bike and Ship section of this book.

By air

To reach your destination by air is another possibility. Many airlines fly to Vienna´s airport in Schwechat, including some low-budget companies. Always check with the individual airlines to determine how the bicycle must be packed, and what additional costs may be charged. From the airport take the CAT (City Airport Train) to Wien-Mitte train station. From there take a right and cycle along the Weiskirchner-straße. Take a right turn at the Ring and then go straight to the Urania, the starting point of this tour.

Bicycle transport

Bicycles on trains/as baggage: Rail passengers in **Austria** may bring bicycles on board only those trains that are marked with the 🚲 symbol in the train schedule, and only if they have a valid bicycle ticket and there is sufficient space on the train. It is therefore a good idea to reserve a place in advance.

In **Hungary** you may bring your bicycle on board most trains, excluding some of the IC-connections. Prices vary according to the length of your trip. Places for bikes should be reserved in advance. Transporting a bicycle from Budapest back to Austria costs about € 10,-/HUF 2460,-. You need an International

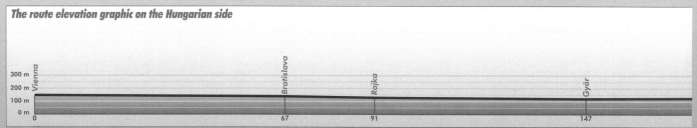

The route elevation graphic on the Hungarian side

Bicycle Ticket which you can buy at Keleti train station in Budapest. If you want to board the train with your bicycle, be prepared to be at the train station an hour in advance.

Taking your bike on Budapest´s subway system is only permitted with a separate bicycle ticket and only at designated places at the train station.

In the **Slovak Republic** you can usually take your bicycles on trains with a luggage waggon. Note that you have to load and unload your bicycle by yourself. On the international connections between Bratislava and Vienna bicycles are only permitted on certain trains, please check in advance with the Slovakian Rail.

To ship a bicycle by rail in Austria, the ÖBB offers a door to door service (Haus-Haus-Gepäck-PLUS-Service). You can book at larger train stations, travel agencies with train ticket sale or call ☎ 051717. The price includes pickup, delivery, and 800 € insurance per luggage item. Sending in Austria is € 14.90. Sending to other European countries costs € 29.90. Please be sure to check fares before booking.

Bike & Ship

Hydrofoil boats provide daily passenger service on the Danube between Vienna and Budapest. A one-way ticket costs € 79. The trip takes about 5-and-a-half hours. These boats will take bicycles if space is available and a reservation is made in advance. A ticket for the bicycle costs € 18.

Departure times in the off-season (April and September-October):
- 9 a.m. in both Vienna and Budapest
Departure times in the main-season:
- 8 a.m. in both Vienna and Budapest.
Check-in one hour before departure.

For more information about Hungarian passenger ships on the Danube contact MAHART, Handelskai 265, Reichsbrücke, A-1021 Wien, ☎ (0)1/7292161, 7292162.

Between Esztergom and Budapest you have the option of switching to "normal" vessels. These will also take bicycles if sufficient space is available. A one-way ticket from Budapest to

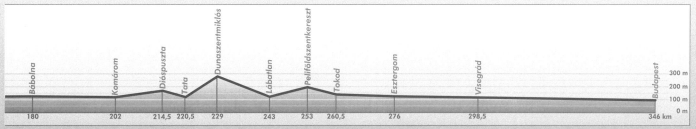

Esztergom costs € 6.10/HUF 1490. Attractive discounts are available. Bicycle transport costs € 2.55/HUF 600. Between May and September, the ship departs Esztergom at 4 p.m. (arrival Budapest about 7:55 p.m.) or Budapest-Batthyány tér at 7:35 a.m. and 9.05 a.m. (the 9:05 a.m. ship only goes as far as Visegrád). The trip takes about 5-and-a-half hours upstream, and about 4 hours downstream. Further information is available at the ship station Info Budapest, Vigadó Platz, ☎ (0)1/3181223, or from Mahart Passnave Schifffahrt, Belgrád rakpart, H-1056 Budapest, ☎ (0)1/4844-014.

Bicycle rentals

Vienna rental stations:

- **Hochschaubahn**, 2. Bezirk (Second District), Prater at the Hochschaubahn, ☎ (0)1/7295888
- **Pedal Power**, 2. Bezirk, Ausstellungsstr. 3, ☎ (0)1/7297234
- **Radverleih City**/Hundertwasserhaus, 3. Bezirk, Kegelg. 37-39, ☎ (0)1/9617771
- **Riebl Sport**, 5. Bezirk, Schönbrunnerstr. 63, ☎ (0)1/5447534
- **Ostbahnbrücke**, 22. Bezirk, at Lobau train station, ☎ 0664/9743718
- **Radverleih Copa Cagrana**, 22. Bezirk, Donauinsel (Danube island) at the Reichsbrücke, ☎ (0)1/2635242
- **Radsport Nußdorf**, 19. Bezirk, Donaupromenade/ at the cycle path, ☎ (0)1/ 3704598
- **Donauinsel/Floridsdorfer Brücke**, 21. Bezirk, ☎ (0)1/2788698

You can also contact the regional tourist offices or bike tour operators for more information.

Overnight accommodations

In many of the towns and villages along the route through Hungary it is easy to find inexpensive accommodations in private homes. These also often offer a good breakfast for an additional price. Reservations for rooms are usually necessary only in the main season, and can be made in the local county seat. In Budapest it is always a good idea to reserve a room in advance. In emergencies, one can rely on the great hospitality of the Hungarian people. Hotels are usually expensive and

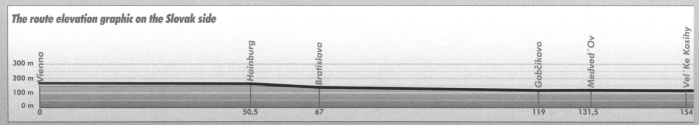

The route elevation graphic on the Slovak side

well-equipped. Guesthouses are considerably more affordable, clean and comfortable. Overnight accommodations in Slovakia are harder to find. Local tourism offices and travel agents have little information about the areas along the Danube.

Bicycle tours with children

The absence of bicycle paths on much of the Danube bicycle route between Vienna and Budapest and the necessity of riding some longer stretches with considerable traffic mean this tour should probably not be undertaken with children under the age of 12. This applies, however, only for the parts in Hungary. In Austria and in Slovakia as far as Medved'ov it is easily possible to ride with small children on the paved path on the causeway along the river.

Bicycling in Vienna

The bicycle trails and lanes in Vienna have their peculiarities, as you will see. Here are some of the most important rules:
Bicyclists must yield the right of way at the end of the bicycle trail, or when leaving any bicycling facility (bicycle path, bicycle lane, multi-purpose lane or bicycle crossing)! At bicycle crossings (marked on the pavement), the bicyclist has the right of way but may not ride faster than 10 km/h! On one-way streets (Einbahnstrasse), bicyclists may ride against the flow only where this is explicitly permitted. In Vienna's pedestrian zones (Fussgänger-zone), bicyclists must dismount and push their vehicle.

Bicycles in public transportation

U-Bahn: Mon-Fri 9-15 and after 18:30, Sun/Hol all day. On the U6 line, bicycles may be transported only in the special low-floor wagons, and may be entered only at doors marked with the bicycle symbol. Half-price ticket: € 0.80.

Schnellbahn (commuter trains): Bicycles may be transported at all times only on trains shown with the bicycle symbol on posted train schedules. One-day tickets cost € 2.90.

Bicycle tour operators

Austria Radreisen, 4780 Schärding,

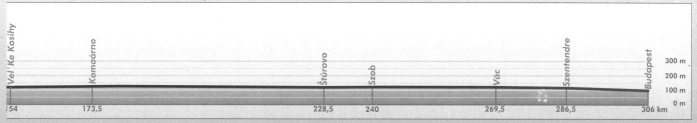

☎ 07712/55110, www.austria-radreisen.at

Donau Radfreunde, Ronthal 2,
A-4090 Engelhartszell, ☎ 077178182,
Fax (0)7717/81827,
E-Mail: donauradfreunde@aon.at,
www.donauradfreunde.com

Eurobike, 5162 Obertrum,
☎ 06219/7444, www.eurobike.at

Pedalo, Zelli 4, A-4712 Michaelnbach,
☎ 0043/7248/635840,
Fax (0)7248/635844,
E-Mail: info@pedalo.com, www.pedalo.com

Rad & Reisen, 1220 Wien,
☎ 01/40538730, www.fahrradreisen.at

Fahrrad-Klinik, D-94032 Passau,
☎ 0851/33411, www.fahrrdklinik-passau.de

Pedalo Radtours Passau, D-94032 Passau,
☎ 0851/32124, www.pedaloradtours.de

Velociped Fahrradreisen,
D-35039 Marburg, ☎ 06421/886890,
info@velociped.de, www.velociped.de

Reisen & Radeln, Kirchheimer Str. 254,
D-73252 Lenningen-Brucken,
☎ (0)7026/600156, Fax (0)7026/600157,
E-Mail: info@reisen-radeln.de, www.reisen-radeln.de

Rückenwind Reisen GmbH,
Industriehof 3, D-26133 Oldenburg,
☎ (0)441/485970, Fax (0)4414859722,
E-Mail: info@rueckenwind.de,
www.rueckenwind.de

Velotours Touristik, CH-78467 Konstanz,
☎ 0041/7531/98280, www.velotours.de

Velo-Touring, Budapest (H),
☎ (0)1 3190571;

The right bicycle

The Danube route can be ridden on just about any functioning bicycle between Vienna and Komárno or Vienna and Györ. From Komárom or Györ to Esztergom we recommend a touring or trekking bikes which is more comfortable on the unpaved parts of the path and lets you cope more easily with the increasing gradient. It is advisable to bring basic tools and accessories.

About this book

This bicycle tour guide includes all the information you need for a vacation riding a bicycle along the Danube: precise maps, large-scale maps of cities and towns, a detailed route description, and information about tourist facilities and sights.

The maps

The inside of the guide's front cover shows an overview of the geographic location area covered by the guide. It also depicts the area covered by each of the detail maps inside the guide, and the detail map's number. These detail maps are produced in a scale of 1:75,000 (1 centimeter = 750 meters). In addition to exactly describing the route, these maps also provide information about roadway quality (paved or unpaved), climbs (gentle or steep), distances, as well as available cultural sites and tourism facilities.

Note that the recommended main route is always shown in red or purple; alternative routes and side trips are shown in orange. The individual symbols used in the maps are described in the legend on page 4.

Route elevation graphic

The route elevation graphic provides an overview of the location of important towns and major ascents and descents along the route. The graphic only shows major changes in elevation, not every single small incline. Major climbs and descents are also indicated with arrows on the individual maps.

The text

The text consists primarily of detailed route descriptions. While these are especially useful in populated areas, the text cannot replace the maps as the tourist's main reference for orientation. The descriptions follow the main recommended route downstream along the Danube. Key phrases about the route description are indicated with the   symbol.

This main text is interrupted by passages describing alternative and excursion routes. These are printed on a light orange background.

To aid in orientation, the names of main towns and villages are printed in bold type. Important points of interest in towns and places are listed and include addresses, telephone numbers and opening times. In large cities we have only included a limited selection of noteworthy sights.

Descriptions of the larger towns and cities, as well as historic, cultural and natural landmarks help round out the travel experience. These paragraphs are printed in italics to distinguish them from the route description.

You will also find paragraphs printed in purple or orange ink to help draw attention to special features:

Text printed in purple indicates that you must make a decision about how your tour shall continue. For instance, there may be an alternative route to another destination or the recommended route deviates from posted route markers.

Furthermore the purple text suggests possible excursions to points of interest or recreational facilities that do not lie directly on the cycling route.

Vienna to Bratislava

67 km

The first stage of the bicycle tour takes you along posted bicycle routes through extensive flood-plains. The old woods are criss-crossed by forgotten arms of the Danube and small ponds and lakes that help irrigate the impenetrable thickets of willows, gray alder, liana, bushes and grasses. The verdant underbrush offers a rich habitat to countless species of animals and insects, forming a biotope which is unique in Europe. On your way out of Vienna, ride through the famous Prater and Lobau, then follow the Hubertusdamm through the Stopfenreuther and the Hainburg flood plain to the small city of Hainburg. From Hainburg one can easily take the bicycle to visit the ruins of the ancient Roman city of Carnuntum, before setting off through the Hainburg Gate to cross into Slovakia and arrive in the young nation's charming capital, Bratislava.

This part of the trip follows marked bicycle paths and good quality tracks on the tops of the flood-barriers. Special caution should be exercised on the city streets in Vienna, along the B9 road near Wolfsthal and at the border crossing to Slovakia.

Tip: The bikeline Bicycle Atlas for Vienna (in German only) can help you navigate the Austrian capital. Maps show the entire city area in a scale of 1:15,000. Riders who are less comfortable on busy city streets may consider using the subways (U-bahn), which permit bicycles Monday through Friday between 9 a.m. and 3 p.m. and after 6:30 p.m, on Saturdays after 9 a.m., and all day on Sunday and holidays. A separate half-price ticket must be purchased for each bicycle.

Vienna ≈km 1929

Telephone area code: 01

🛈 **Tourist Information**, 1., Albertinaplatz/corner of Maysedergasse

🛈 **Vienna tourism**, ☏ 21114

🏛 **Albertina**, 1, Albertinapl. 1, ☏ 534830, Open: Daily 10-18, Weds 10-21. Rotating exhibitions of international art from the renaissance to the contemporary. One of the largest art collections in the world, with works by Dürer, Leonardo, Raffael, Michelangelo, Schiele, Cézanne, Klimt, Kokoschka, Picasso, Rauschenberg and many others, from the 15th century to today. Dürer's original "Rabbit" and "Praying Hands" are located in the Albertina

🏛 **Art history museum (Kunsthistorisches Museum)**, 1, Maria Theresien Platz, ☏ 525240, comprises main building, Neue Burg and Palais Harrach. Open: Tues-Sun 10-18, Thurs 10-21. One of the most renowned art collections in the world. The core collection includes works by Dürer, Rubens, Titian, and Bruegel the older (largest Bruegel collection in the world). Also noteworthy: the

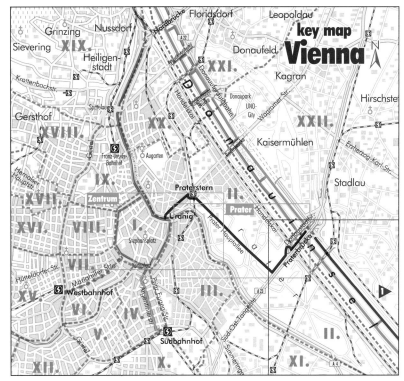

Egyptian/Oriental collection, antiquity collections and numismatics collection.

- 🏛 **Natural history museum (Naturhistorisches Museum)**, 1, Maria Theresien Platz, ✆ 521770, Open: Mon, Weds-Sun 9-18:30, Weds 9-21. Includes minerals, rare uncut diamonds and meteorites, a fossil collection and 15,000 skeletons (including dinosaurs). Prehistoric items include the original "Willendorf Venus" and anthropological items from the early-Paleolithic period to the present. Roof tours Weds 17 o'clock and 18:30 by appointment at ✆ 52177320.

- 🏛 **Austrian museum of applied arts (Österreichisches Museum für angewandte Kunst)**, 1, Stubenring 5, ✆ 711360, Open: Tues 10-24, Weds-Sun 10-18. Collections range from antiquity to the Middle Ages to the contemporary, and include glass, ceramics, metalworks, furniture, porcelain, textiles, oriental rugs and east-Asian crafts as well as Viennese art nouveau items.

- 🏛 **KunstHausWien**, 3, Untere Weißgerberstr. 13, ✆ 7120491, Open: Mon-Sun 10-19, guided tours Sun/Hol 11 and 12 o'clock or by appointment, ✆ 712049512. Works by Hundertwasser (painting, architecture, sculpture) and visiting exhibitions by 20th century artists.

- 🏛 **Kunsthalle Wien**, 4, Karlsplatz/Treitlstr. 2, ✆ 5218914, Open: Mon-Sun 13-19. Rotating exhibitions of contemporary

Vienna

art and masterpieces of classical modernism.

- 🏛 **Das Museumsquartier**, Museumspl. 1, Info at ✆ 5235881. The Vienna Museum Quarter with 60,000 square meters of exhibition space is one of the 10 largest art districts in the world. Includes major art collections like the Leopold Museum, contemporary spaces like Kunsthalle Vienna and the Festival of the Vienna Festwochen. The Museumsquartier offers old masters and modern art, baroque and Cyberspace, fantasy voyages and recreation in the center of the Austrian capital.

- 🏛 **Treasure chamber (Schatzkammer)**, 1, Hofburg-Schweizerhof, ✆ 525240, Mon, Weds-Sun 10-18. One of the world's greatest treasure troves, includes the Holy Roman Emperor's crown (c. 962), the Austrian Emperor's crown, the

Burgundy treasure and the treasures of the Order of the Golden Fleece.

- 🏛 **Österreichische Galerie Belvedere**, 3, Oberes Belvedere, Prinz Eugen Str. 27, ✆ 79557134, Open: Tues-Sun 10-18. A collection of Austrian art, ranging from Biedermeier to the Ringstraßen period to art nouveau. Artists represented include Klimt, Schiele and Kokoschka as well as Waldmüller, Romako, Makart, Wotruba and others.

- 🏛 **Sigmund Freud Museum**, 9, Bergg. 19, ✆ 3191596, Open: July-Sept., Mon-Sun 9-18, Oct.-June, Mon-Sun 9-17. Guided tours if signed up ahead. The founder of psychoanalysis lived here from 1891 until he was forced to leave in 1938. Freud's former medical office is set us as a museum.

- 🏛 **Secession**, 1, Friedrichstr. 12, ✆ 5875307, Open: Tues-Sun/Hol 10-18, Thurs 10-20. Built 1897-98 according to plans by Joseph Olbrich for the "Viennese Secession" group of progressive artists. Rotating exhibitions of modern art plus the 34-meter Beethoven frieze by Gustav Klimt.

- ♿ **St. Stephan's cathedral**, 1 Stephansplatz, ✆ 51552-3767, Guided tours: Mon-Sat 10:30 and 15, Sun/Hol 15 o'clock. Austria's most important Gothic structure and, along with the Prater Ferris-wheel, a Vienna landmark that represents 800 years of history. Noteworthy: the red marble gravestone for Kaiser Frederick III, Anton Pilgram's pulpit (1514-

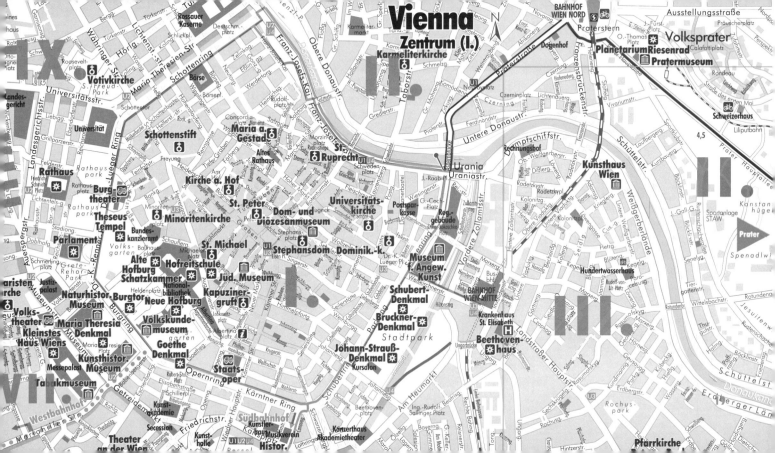

1515), the Viennese "Neustädter Altar" (1447). Guided tours of the extensive catacombs under the cathedral: Mon-Sat 10-11:30 and 13:30-16:30, Sun/Hol 13:30-16:30.

🔷 **Schönbrunn palace**, 13, Schönbrunner Schlossstraße (U-Bahn Station), ✆ 81113305, Open: Fri, Sat 13-17, Sun/Hol 10-17, groups by appointment Mon-Fri 9-13, Mon-Sun 10-17 during Austrian school vacation. Original plans by Fischer von Erlach, who proposed a palace that would be larger and more magnificent than Versailles. Built 1696-1730, with 1,441 rooms and chambers. Served as Habsburg summer residence and venue of the Congress of Vienna.

🔷 **Belvedere**, upper and lower Alpine gardens, Austrian Belvedere Gallery, 3, Prinz Eugen Str. 27, ✆ 79557134, Open: Tues-Sun 10-18. The palace is regarded as one of the most beautiful baroque structures. Built 1700 by Lukas von Hildebrandt as a summer residence for Prince Eugene of Savoy. Includes an elegant terraced garden with cascades and sculptures.

✳ **Spanish Riding school**, 1, Hofburg, Josefsplatz, ✆ 534100, Information available at www.spanische-reitschule.com

✳ **Ringstraße.** The old city defensive fortifications were demolished 1857-58 and replaced by a beautiful boulevard now lined with buildings that include the Burg theater, Museum of Art History and the Parliament. The bourgeois also erected a monumental structure, the Palais.

✳ **Spittelberg.** The neighborhood between Breite Gasse and Stiftgasse provides an example of how an historic (in this case Biedermeier period) area can be preserved and revitalized. Today a popular and lively artists' quarter with flair.

✳ **Naschmarkt**, Wienzeile between Getreidemarkt and Kettenbrückengasse. Vienna's largest fruit and vegetable market, full of individuality and atmosphere, is the living antithesis of modern supermarkets. Large flea market on Saturdays.

✳ Ferris wheel (Riesenrad) in the Prater. Open: Nov, Dec, Jan, Feb 10-20; March, April & Oct, 10-22, May-Sept, 9-24. Built 1896/97 by the engineer Walter Basset, with 61 meter diameter.

✳ **Rad & U-Bahn**. Mon-Fri 9-15 and after 18:30, Sat after 9, all day Sun/Hol. A half-price ticket must be purchased for the bicycle. Enter subway cars only at doors marked with the bicycle symbol. On the U 6 line only in cars with low floors.

✳ **Rad & Schnellbahn**. Mon-Fri 9-15 and after 18:30, Sat after 9, all day Sun/Hol. Bicycles may be brought on board of all trains that are shown in the schedules with a bicycle symbol. In Vienna's central zone (Zone 100) it is necessary to purchase a half-price ticket for the bicycle. For all other trains purchase a bicycle day-ticket.

✳ **Guided bicycle tours**: Pedal Power Tours, Ausstellungsstr. 3, ✆ 7297234. Discovery rides through Vienna, 1 May to 30 Sept.

✳ **Vienna ticket (Wien-Karte)**, 72-hour ticket valid for all forms of public transportation, includes discounts to many museums and other sights. Available from Tourist Information offices, many hotels and ticket-offices at larger U-Bahn stations.

🔷 **Zoo – Tiergarten Schönnbrunn**, Schlosspark near Hietzinger Tor (U-Bahn), ✆ 87792940, Open: Nov-Jan, Mon-Sun 9-16:30, Feb, Mon-Sun 9-17, March, Oct, Mon-Sun 9-17:30, April, Mon-Sun 9-18, May-Sept, Mon-Sun 9-18:30. The world's oldest zoo, set in a baroque park, with many innovative ideas for keeping animals.

Some of the stereotypes about Vienna focus on its inhabitants' alleged smug complacency, snide humor and melancholy aloofness. But a look behind the faded luster of the one-time imperial capital's facade reveals a surprisingly modern and multi-facetted metropolis. Today's Vienna combines a vibrant cultural landscape, international diplomacy, and the interaction of peoples from around the world.

Beneath the travel brochures' sugar-frosted descriptions of a charming old European capital, there teems a lively and many-sided city of contrasts. The cranky old man next to the Kaiser Franz Josef monument in the Burggarten who peddles postcards bearing the Emperor's likeness is as much a part of the city's face as the "Fiaker" drivers, all set against the backdrop of a city center characterized by the 19th century edifices whose attention-seeking magnificence betrays the superficiality that in the end contributed to the Empire's collapse.

It was also the Kaiser who resisted the modern forces and influences that coursed through turn-of-the-century Europe. Otto Wagner, the influential city planner of the period, built the tram-stations that represented the first forays into styles of architecture that dispensed with the established conservative conventions. His functional structures today form central elements of the city's public transportation system.

He was followed by Adolf Loos, whose architectural ambitions united all the fin de siècle influences. He was the Karl Kraus of public buildings, who set his buildings into the cityscape like statements, including one directly in front of the Kaiser's bedroom window. The architect coolly went ahead with his Loos Haus on the Michaelerplatz, which today houses a bank, despite the warning attributed to Kaiser Franz Josef: "Loos will have to build that thing over by dead body."

Rathaus, Vienna

Loos and Wagner left the most distinctive marks on the city in the period immediately after the turn of the century. The "red Vienna" of the 1920s helped drive a boom in municipal construction projects. There is not a district in the city which does not feature examples of the socialist residential projects. The most famous of these is the Karl Marx Hof in the 19th district.

World War II also left its mark on the city: Much of the city was destroyed and had to be rebuilt, but the enormous "flak-towers" on which anti-aircraft cannons were mounted, have resisted all demolition attempts. One of these huge reinforced-concrete structures in the 6th district now houses the "Haus des Meeres" aquarium.

There are numerous other significant buildings in the city as well, including the futuristic "UNO-city" which has put Vienna on the world's international diplomacy map, the Danubeturm, the buildings of Friedensreich Hundertwasser (including the apartment building on Löwengasse and the waste-incinerator Spittelau), the Haas Haus (which critics say provides a poor counterpoint to the venerable cathedral across the Stephansplatz), the Millenium Tower and the Andromeda Tower near UNO City.

Away from the city's bustle, Vienna of-fers many colorful plazas and squares. The "Naschmarkt" near the Opera is Vienna's largest and most varied food and produce market. It is joined by a large flea-market on Saturdays. Art and artists can be found around the Markt am Spittelberg in the 7th district, where urban-renewal efforts have not completely eliminated the neighborhood's somewhat seedier bohemian atmosphere. Spittelberg used to be seen as Vienna's shabbiest quarter, a place populated with drug users and prostitutes. Today it is quieter, with organic food stores and astrology shops mixed among the remaining smoky pubs and recently renovated buildings.

Vienna is still said to lie on the banks of the Danube, yet to actually see the river now one must leave the old city, which now only has the Danube Canal. The city lost its direct access to the river in the 19th century, when the main stream was moved northward to end the danger posed by flooding. In more recent times a parallel canal (Neue Danube) was

Ferris wheel in the Prater

dug next to the Danube, with the excavated fill used to create the 21-kilometer Danube island, which has since become one of Vienna' most popular recreation areas. Once a year it is also the venue for the "Donauinselfest" – the city's annual mega-party.

Vienna to Orth a. d. Danube	30 km

Wiener Prater

The ancient trees, tranquil waters, game re-serves and the Lusthaus at the end of the main avenue have characterized Vienna's Prater for centuries. "The Vienna Prado", as the royal

hunting grounds were known, stretched more than 10 kilometers along the Danube. The Wurstelprater, or People's Prater, dates to April 7, 1766, when the enlightened Kaiser Joseph II for the first time opened the Praterauen, or flood-plains, to the public. The first refresh-ment stands, or Wurstelbuden, soon opened, and were quickly followed by restaurants and beer gardens, bowling lanes, carousels and a puppet-theatre. The first fireworks display came in 1771, and 20 years later Jean-Pierre Blanchard launched a gas-filled balloon from the Prater.

Coffee-houses established along the main avenue quickly became a famous part of the Prater's attractions, and were especially popular before the first world war. In 1945 the Wurstelprater was almost completely de-stroyed by fire during the battle for Vienna. Only 18 objects survived, and the Wurst-elprater has never been the same since. Today it is a collection of carousels, casinos and snack-bars. What little is left of the old Wurstelprater, like the Calafati Carousel and

the "Big Chinaman", can be found in the less gaudy areas to the rear of the park.

The Viennese always distinguished between the People's Prater and the "Nobelprater" which, with the exception of the race-track in Freudenau, had no carnival atmosphere. An extensive park with long lanes and paths, carefully tended landscapes as well as areas of wild growth that recalled its origins as a royal hunting grounds, this was where the city's young lovers would come to find some privacy, where retirees came to stroll, and where governesses brought their charges to play. It was, of course, also where high society gathered to see and be seen, mounted or in coaches, especially on the first of May, for the traditional "Praterfahrt" to celebrate arrival of the spring. People without horse or buggy came out as well, to watch the colorful spectacle, criticise the moneyed classes or review the latest summer fashions being shown for the first time. Starting in 1886, the Hauptallee served as the venue for a flower parade with horse-drawn carriages. Eleven years later a flower parade for cyclists was introduced, as was one for automobiles after World War I.

Today the Prater serves Viennese and tourists as an amusement park, a place to eat and drink, a vast garden for long walks and quiet picnics. For a first-time visitor, no day at the Prater could be complete without a ride on the giant ferris wheel, which affords a spectacular view across the city.

Proceed along the Autobahn that cuts through the Prater to the Praterbrücke ~ the bridge has a bicycle path ~ cross the Donauinsel, which is a weekend paradise for Vienna's bicyclists.

Take the bicycle path along the **Neue Danube** to the oil terminal ~ cross the refinery road.

Tip: You can turn left here to reach the Lobau Museum.

Lobau

🏛 **Lobaumuseum**, Vorwerk 1, ✆ 02214/3571, Open: Weds 9-12, Mon-Tues and Thurs-Fri 13-15:30, guided tours Sun/Hol 13-17 by appointment. Six rooms of exhibits about the Lobau environment and the adjacent Danube flood plains (Donauauen). 320 displays presenting the region's flora and fauna.

Turn onto **Lobgrundstraße** and ride past the ÖMV oil storage tanks ~ and enter the old forest of the Lobau.

Tip: The forest is swarming with waterbirds, wild animals and rare creatures that thrive on the forest's natural ecosystem. During high-water the route may be closed, in which case riders face a longer detour.

The **Hubertusdamm (which is also known as the Marchfelddamm)** is about 30 kilometers long ~ the causeway path is almost entirely paved ~ just before Schönau a bridge crosses a branch of the Danube.

Tip: Riders suffering from thirst or hunger can find replenishment at the "Zur alten Fähre" inn, which can be reached by riding a short distance towards the village of Schönau.

Ride straight along the causeway through the river flood plains ~ after 7 kilometers you reach an intersection.

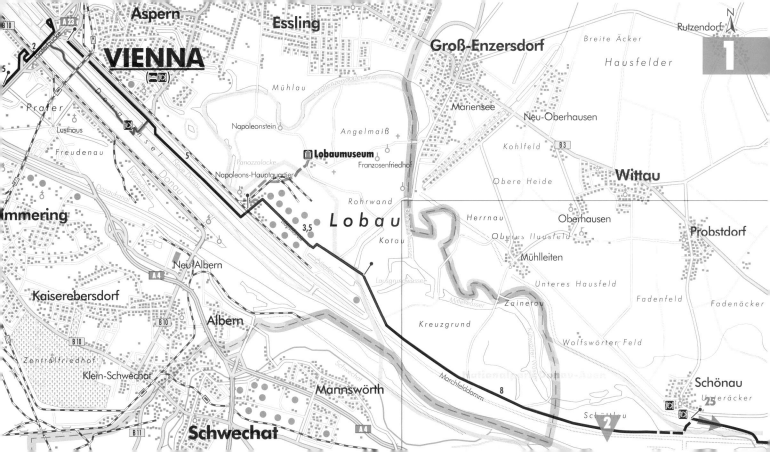

Aspern

Essling

Groß-Enzersdorf

Rutzendorf

Breite Äcker

Hausfelder

VIENNA

Mühlau

Mariensee

Neu-Oberhausen

Kohlfeld

B 3

Prater

Napoleonstein

Angelmaiß

Wittau

Lusthaus

Franzosenfriedhof

Obere Heide

Oberhausen

Freudenau

Panozzalacke

🏛 Lobaumuseum

Probstdorf

Napoleons-Hauptquartier

Rohrwand

Herrnau

Lobau

Oberes Hausfeld

Simmering

Mühlleiten

Kotau

Neu-Albern

3,5

Unteres Hausfeld

Fadenfeld

Fadenäcker

A 4

Lausgrundwasser

Kaiserebersdorf

Zainetau

Albern

B 10

Kreuzgrund

Wolfswörter Feld

B 10

Mittelwasser

Zentralfriedhof

Schönau

Klein-Schwechat

Marchfelddamm

8

Unteräcker

25

Mannswörth

2

Schwechat

B 11

A 4

Schütlau

Tip: Here you can either turn right and ride to the Danube and the Schiffmühle or turn left to Orth a. d. Donau for a delightful side-trip to a town noted for its excellent fish.

Orth a. d. Danube

Postal code: 2304; Phone area code: 02212

🛈 **Town office**, Am Markt 26, ✆ 2208, www.orth.at

⛴ **Orth-Haslau** ferry, ✆ 2481, Open: April-Oct, Mon-Sun 9 to sunset.

🏛 **Fishing and Danube river museum** (Fischerei- and Donaumuseum), Schloss Orth, ✆ 2555, Open: Tues-Sun 9-12 and 13-17, Danube museum by appointment.

🏛 **Beekeeping and local history museum** (Bienenzucht- and Heimatmuseum), Schloss Orth, ✆ 2555, Open: Tues-Sun 9-12 and 13-17. Beekeeping and local history.

🏰 **Schloss Orth**, massive medieval castle, first mentioned in 865.

✳ **Schiffmühle**, this floating mill is the only functioning mill on the entire Danube. It uses the river's current to grind every kind of grain. It lies some 300 meters from the Uferhaus fish restaurant, on the other side of a branch of the river. Access to the mill on a historic Danube boat. The mill is open from 30 March to 2 November. Boat rides to the mill

Carnuntum Roman site

from the Uferhaus boat landing at 14 o'clock, and 11-14 Sun/Hol, and by appointment.

🚲 **Erwin Fuchs**, Hauptstr. 14, ✆ 2362, 2326

Three museums are located in the late-Gothic castle in Orth, in the middle of the National park March-Donauauen. They are the fishing museum, which documents the long tradition of fishing in the Danube, the Danube museum with its history of the river, and a beekeeping museum.

Orth a. d. Danube to Hainburg   20.5 km

Tip: About half-way along the Hubertusdamm one comes to the baroque Eckartsau hunting lodge. A visit is always worthwhile.

Eckartsau

Postal code: 2305; Phone area code: 02214

🛈 **Town office**, Obere Hauptstr.1, ✆ 2202, www.marktgemeinde-eckartsau.at

🏰 **Eckartsau baroque palace**, ✆ 22400, Open: Sat, Sun/Hol 8-16, Tours at 11 and 13, weekdays by appointment

🏨 **Kaltenbrunner**, Obere Hauptstr. 22, ✆ 2226

The former river castle was converted to a hunting lodge by Count Kinsky in 1722. It includes statues and reliefs by Lorenzo Matielli as well as frescoes by Daniel Gran. This castle is closely associated with the last chapter of the Austro-Hungarian empire.

Just before the end of the causeway, pass the Stopfenreuth forest inn and then turn on to the bridge across the Danube.

Stopfenreuth

Postal code: 2292; Phone area code: 02214

🛈 **Engelhartstetten town office**, Obere Hauptstr. 2, ✆ 2292

✳ **Forsthaus Stopfenreuth**, ✆ 2232, Open: year-round, Mon-Sun. Floodplain information center with food and bicycle service.

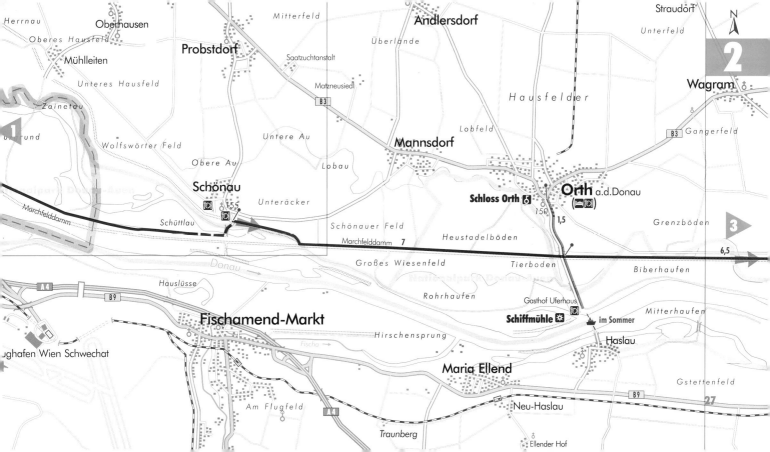

Floatin mill near Orth

✿ **Pranger** am Anger, from the 16th century.

Stoptenreuth and Bad Deutsch Altenburg are connected by an imposing suspension bridge. The resort town of Bad Deutsch Altenburg has mineral baths.

Take the unpaved track on the dike straight to the bridge ⌁ proceed under the bridge ⌁ then immediately left and up to the main road ⌁ cross the main road ⌁ and next to the right side across the long suspension bridge ⌁ at the end of the bridge turn right away from the road ⌁ to another crossing street ⌁ turn right ⌁ towards Bad Deutsch Altenburg.

Bad Deutsch Altenburg

Postal code: 2405; Phone area code: 02165

ℹ️ **Tourism office**, Bad Deutsch-Altenburg resort office, Erhardg. 2, ✆ 62900

🏛 **Archaeological Museum Carnuntum**, Open: Jan- March, Sat 11-17, Tues-Sun 10-17. Subjects: Roman tools, jewelry, weapons, armor and other artifacts.

🔳 **St. Mary's church** (Marienkirche). One of the oldest churches in lower Austria stands on a hill in the town. The main building probably dates to about 1000. The church was expanded in the Romanesque style at a later date. In the 14th century the tower and a Gothic choir were added.

✿ **Amphitheater**, Open: Late March-early Nov, Mon-Sun 9-17

Bad Deutsch Altenburg is a resort town with modern facilities and the strongest iodine-sulfur baths in Austria, in the "Archaeological Park Carnuntum." The town lies in the Pannonic region of Austria and is one of the sunniest parts of the country. Two-thousand years ago the Romans built a thermal baths at the same site.

Excursion to Carnuntum   4.5 km

Hobby archaeologists will especially relish a visit to the Archeological Park Carnuntum, which has some of the most important Roman excavations in Austria. It is located in Petronell, 4 kilometers from Bad Deutsch Altenburg.

The easiest way to reach Petronell-Carnuntum from Bad Deutsch-Altenburg is on the Roman road.

Petronell-Carnuntum

Postal code: 2404; Phone area code: 02163

ℹ️ **Town office**, Kirchenpl. 1, ✆ 2228

🏛 **Petronell Roman museum** (Römer-Museum der Marktgemeinde Petronell), Hauptstr. 439, ✆ 2780, Open: May-Sept, Sat, Sun/Hol 10-16 or by appointment. Subject: Types of graves, burial objects, an underground water conduit, special exhibitions.

🏛 **Petronell** open air museum (Freilichtmuseum), Open: Late March-early Nov, Mon-Sun 9-17

🔳 **Count Abenberg-Traunsche palace**. Originally built as a river castle, reconfigured in the 17th century by the baroque master D. Carlone.

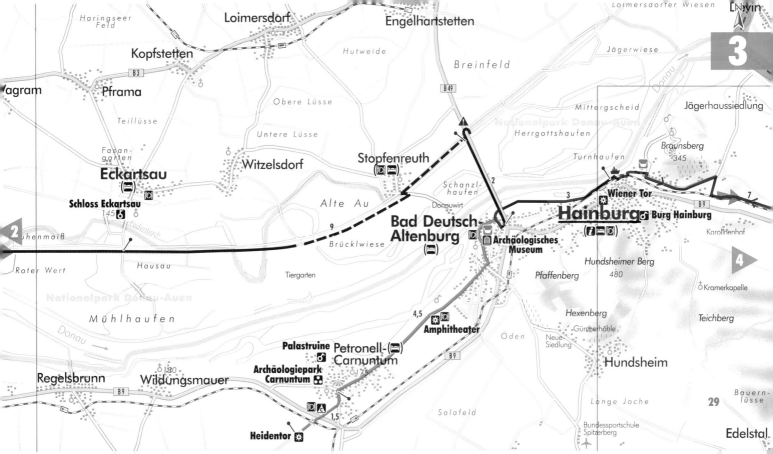

⊠ Carnuntum archaeological park (Archäologischer Park Carnuntum), Hauptstr. 3, ✆ 33770. The largest archaeological park in Austria, divided into three main areas: a museum district, the legion camp, and the civilian town.

🚉 Bahnhof Petronell-Carnuntum, ✆ 2290

Silvery-green poplars line the street that leads from Vienna to the Roman excavations at Carnuntum. The road from Vienna to Bratislava follows the route of the Via Principalis, upon which ancient peoples could travel all the way to Rome without a visa. With a little imagination, one can see in the poplars a similarity to the cypress trees that line the Via Appia, and picture a Roman structure every hill.

The origins of the provincial Roman capital go back much further. In the times of the Illyrians and Celts two ancient trading roads intersected here – the Danube from west to east and the Amber Road, which connected the Mediterranean and the Baltic seas. During the reign of Caesar Tiberius the city Carnuntum (which mean city on the stone) was incorporated into the province of Pannonia.

Danube and Hainburg from the Braunsberg

The camp's strategic importance triggered a period of great prosperity.

In 171 AD the Marcomans invaded and destroyed the city. Marcus Aurelius recaptured Carnuntum and rebuilt it, before it eventually fell to the Huns. In the ensuing dark periods of migrations the city slowly died. The Huns were followed by the Eastgoths and the Avars. No one recorded the city's final downfall, perhaps because the enemy left no survivors living. In one oven archaeologists found the remains of half-finished bread, as if the Roman baker did not even have time to remove the bread from the oven.

What the Germanic tribes and forces of natural decay did not destroy was dismantled and carried away by humans. Left standing were the massive pillars of the Heidentor (Heathen's Gate). Extensive research appears to have finally revealed its secret: it is neither a gate nor of heathen origin, but one of four entrances to a monumental victory monument erected for Caesar Constantine II around 354-361 AD. At that time Christianity had been the official Roman religion for several decades and was gaining recognition around the Empire. After extensive repairs the gate today is the best-known attraction in the archaeological park.

Tip: A civilian settlement took shape not far from the Roman legions' camp. A ride to the Heidentor leads past numerous remains of the Roman past. If you can tear yourself away from the grip of ancient history, return to the Danube bridge and the road that leads to Budapest.

Proceed straight toward the Danube ～ pass under the bridge ～ and onto Hollitzer Allee

~ and continue straight ~ this road is closed to automobiles. After 2.5 kilometers you reach the Hainburg train station.

Tip: To reach the center of Hainburg one must ride a short distance up from the river.

Hainburg

Postal code: 2410; Phone area code: 02165

🅸 **Town office**, Hauptpl. 23, ✆ 62111, www.hainburg.at

🅸 **Guest information**, ✆ 62111-23

⚓ **Ferry to Devin**, Hainburg ships landing, ✆ 01/7283100

🏛 **City museum in the Vienna gate** (Stadtmuseum im Wienertor), Open: May-Oct, Sun/Hol 10-12 and 14-17. History of Hainburg, including the tobacco factory. Guided tours by appointment ✆ 2111-23.

✳ **Vienna gate** (Wienertor). Built in the 13th century, is regarded as one of the most artistically-significant city gates in central Europe.

✳ **Old city**. With numerous historic city houses, city museum, 11th century and 13th century fortifications.

✉ **Bergbad**, Braunsberger Straße

The medieval city of Hainburg lies above the Danube surrounded by wooded hills in the middle of the Donauauen national park. The 3 city gates and 15 city towers dating to the 13th century are unrivalled in central Europe, and hint that this is one of the most strategic points along the Danube. The earliest recorded mention of Hainburg dates to 1042, and for a long time the city was the main eastern outpost of the Holy Roman Empire.

This is where the Danube winds between the Braunsberg, on the Austrian side, and the Thebener Kogel that looms over the confluence of the March on the Slovakian side. Before 1918 it was called Upper Hungary. At

end of World War I the border moved, making the former Hungarian coronation city the capital of Slovakia. Even so, when one leaves Hainburg towards the east one still does so through the Hungarian Gate, built in 1260.

The imposing 31 meters tall Vienna Gate impresses upon the viewer that these city gates were designed to keep invaders from passing. The gate's opening is small and inconspicuous, weighty is that which solidly surrounds it. The fortified gate was built in 1270 and financed in part with the 100,000 Cologne Marks (about 23,000 kg of silver) ransom that was paid for the release of Richard the Lionhearted. It ranks as one of the most handsome gates of the period, a gate for crusaders and against Hungarian armies – a

Vienna Gate in Hainburg

gate which makes the Dark Ages seem romantic instead of gloomy.

Above the town, on the Schlossberg, can be seen the ruins of an extensive castle which is so ancient that it was already considered old when the Song of the Nibelungen was written.

The walls of Hainburg were repeatedly attacked – although between 1270 and 1481 no enemies tried to conquer the city – but its fortifications remain almost entirely preserved. They stretch from the castle down to the Danube. The narrow Blutgässchen in front of the Fischertor, which opens down to the Danube, hints at the gruesomeness of Hainburg's darkest hours.

When the Turks made their second attempt to push through to Vienna, on July 12, 1683,

the walls of Hainburg, which were in poor condition, could not withstand the onslaught. After a short siege, the Turkish armies stormed the walls. The city's population hoped to escape to the Danube's flood plain, but the doors to the Fischer Gate, which opened inwards, could not be opened in time. Trapped in the narrow passage in front of the gate they were either crushed to death in the panic or fell to the Turks' scimitars. The history of that day reports that 8,432 Hainburgers were killed or taken away by the Turks, and just 100 people escaped. One of them was a young cartwright named Thomas Haydn – a lucky stroke for the world of music: He grew up to become the grandfather of Joseph Haydn.

Today the Fischer Gate no longer blocks the way to the Danube. Instead there is a high embankment on which the railroad passes safe from floodwaters. The line once went as far as Bratislava (or Pressburg in German), but today it stops in the Austrian border village of Wolfsthal.

Hainburg to Bratislava   **17.5 km**

350 meters behind the Hainburg train station ~ ride around the water tower ~ and to the right, under the railroad ~ then left at the intersection and under the railroad tracks again ~ stay to the right ~ along Nibelungengasse ~ and then right into Krüklstraße ~ turn left just before the railroad crossing at the Ungartorbahnhof ~ onto Kriemhildengasse ~ straight ~ then stay left and turn onto Thebenerstraße ~ and ride out of Hainburg ~ you come to a point where several paths branch apart ~ you turn right on a paved asphalt road ~ and proceed straight next to the main road and the railroad line ~ at a row of trees turn left towards the Danube ~ and then follow the bicycle route signs to the right ~ and right, over a small stone bridge, and into Wolfsthal ~ straight ~ to the B9 main road.

Tip: From Hainburg you can take a ferry down the river to the Slovakian town of Devin or continue by bicycle on the Austrian side of the river.

The bicycle path from Hainburg to Wolfsthal is posted. It runs mostly along the railroad ~ just before Wolfsthal turn left down to the floodplain ~ and enter Wolfsthal from the rear ~ turn left at the **B 9** national road.

Wolfsthal-Berg

Postal code: 2412; Phone area code: 02165

🛈 Town office Wolfsthal, Hauptstr. 42, ✆ 62676

🏰 Walterskirchen palace, 17th century

🏰 Pottenburg ruin, on the road to Berg

⛪ „Maria am Birnbaum" pilgrimage church, on the B9 (Hauptstr. 32)

✳ „Immaculate Conception" pillar (Frauensäule „Unbefleckte Empfängnis"), on the B9 near Knaus Park, from 1680

Stay on the main road through Wolfsthal ~ at the eastern end of Wolfsthal the bicycle trail resumes on the left side of the road and leads to the border and on to Bratislava.

Tip: To pass the border one must get on main road and join other travelers at the passport check. In Slovakia the bicycle trail resumes along the causeway on the left. The location of the lanes for motorized traffic make it advisable to immediately go left after the passport check and use the unused lanes to reach the bicycle trail.

The bicycle route goes under the first large bridge.

The bicycle path leads to the first bridge into the city (SNP bridge) on **Viedenska cesta**.

Tip: The bridge has a viewing platform which can be reached by elevator. It offers a fine birds' eye view of the Slovakian capital.

After the bridge proceed straight to a main road ~ you can now see the **Nový Most bridge** ahead of you.

Tip: You can take the bridge across the Danube to reach the center of Bratislava.

Bratislava

Postal code: 82000; Phone area code: 02

🛈 Bratislava Information Service, Klobunicka 2, ✆ 54433715

🏛 Slovakian National Museum (Slov. národné múzeum), Burgpalast, Open: Tues-Sun 9-17

🏛 **Pharmaceutical Museum**, Michalská, Open: Tues-Sun 10-17. The "Red Crab" pharmacy dates back to the 18th century and has comprehensive displays about drugs, including homeopathic medicine.

🏛 **Wine museum** (Vinohradníke múzeum), in the old town hall, Open: Tues-Sun 10-17. Part of the city museum with history of wine production in the region.

🏛 **Clock museum** (Múzeum Hodín), Zidovská ul. 1, Open: Weds-Mon 10-17. The building survived a 1970s urban renewal program that saw much of the Jewish quarter destroyed. Today it is one of the best-preserved rococo structures in Europe.

🏛 **Gallery in the Palais Palffy**, Panská 9, Open: Tues-Sun 10-17. 20th century and contemporary Slovakian art and painters.

🏛 **Slovakian National gallery** (Slov. Národná Galéria), Rázusovo nám., ☎ 02/54434587 Open: Tues-Sun 10-17. Collection includes numerous paintings and sculptures from various periods. Guide tours available by appointment.

🏰 **Hrad**. The 12th century castle was rebuilt in 1430 in the Gothic style and became Hungary's most important fortress. At the time of Maria Theresa a formal palace was added. When Budapest became the Hungarian capital, the castle lost its significance. Today it is the seat of the Slovakian national assembly.

🏰 **Devin castle ruin**, above the confluence of the Danube and March, west of the city. During the reawakening of the Slovakian national identity in the 19th century the ruins were a key symbol of the country's "glorious Slavic past." The fortress played an important military role in the 16th century during the Turkish sieges of Bratislava and Vienna.

⛪ **St. Martins cathedral** (Dom sv. Martina), Rudnayovo nám. 7. The three-nave Gothic building from the 14-15th centuries served as the coronation church for Hungarian kings between 1563 and 1830. It was once remodeled in the baroque style, then returned to its Gothic style in the 19th century. Opulent interior decoration.

⛪ **Franciscan church** (Frantiskánsky kostol), Frantiskanske nám. First consecrated in 1297, remodeled in the baroque style in the 17th and 18th centuries.

✴ **Michael gate**, Michalská ul. The last remaining gate from the original city fortifications. Originally a Gothic construction from the 14th century, today home of a weapons museum.

✴ **Old city hall** (Stará radnica), Hlavne ´ na'm. Gothic building redone in the baroque style, with pretty interior courtyard and tower.

✴ **Slavín memorial**, north-west of the city. Originally built as memorial to Soviet soldiers who died taking the city in 1945, today a monument to the communist period. Excellent views.

The capital of Slovakia, Bratislava, lies flush on the Danube near the western reaches of the Little Carpathian mountains. Originally called Pressburg in German until the end of WWI when the Czechoslovak Republic was established in 1918, the city was renamed after Bratislav, the last leader of the Greater Moravian empire.

Bratislava, which in the past was famous for its watchmakers and clock collections, still bears many traces of the conflicts that helped shape its history. Today's capital of one of the oldest Slavic peoples was for more than 200 years at the center of the Hungarian Empire, until it was almost completely occupied by the Turks after the Battle of Mohács in 1526.

When the Turks left, the Habsburgers came to claim the crown of St. Stefan. At the death of her father, Maria Theresa arrived with her newly-born son to seek the assistance of the

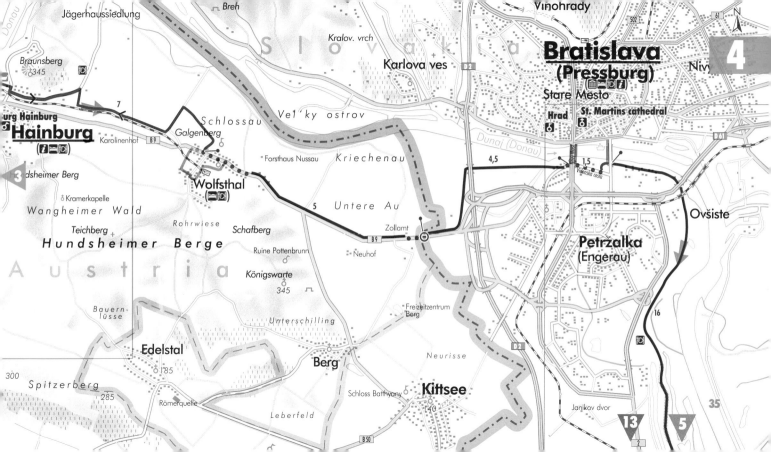

Hungarian nobility to assure the survival of her House. Charles VI had left no male heirs, and of the 63 titles he claimed, the only one which was not contested by others was "King of Hungary." Appealing to the Hungarian magnates at the diet of Pressburg in 1741, she reputedly said, "We have been abandoned by everyone else. Our only refuge are these famous families, their weapons and the heroic spirit of this nation." One of Maria Theresa's trusted knights, Count Janos Pálffy, later recalled the impact of the queen's appearance in Pressburg castle: "... as if possessed by one soul, we drew our swords and swore 'Vitam et sanguinem pro Maiestate Nostra! – Our lives and our blood for our Majesty!' And we wept together with our Queen tears of loyalty, love and indignation." Their support and money helped the young Empress reform government and strength her armies.

Before 1918 the Viennese regarded Pressburg as a quaint suburb, easily reached in less than an hour and notable for its fine white wines.

Bratislava

When one takes a ship today from Vienna to Bratislava, one passes many of the old gentleman ubiquitous to all cities on great rivers – men who despite the weight of their pocketwatches still have time to endlessly fish, philosophize and monitor the river traffic. In Bratislava they stand at the foot of the castle and in the shadow of a unique single-towered suspension bridge across the majestic river. The 431 meter span was built on what was once the Jewish quarter.

The highest point in Bratislava is the television tower visible on the edge of the city where the vineyards and foothills of the Little Carpathians rise from the Danube flood plain.

Bratislava

Slavin memorial

Staré Mesto

nám. Slobody

Slovakian National Council

Hrad

Clock museum

Michael gate (weapons museum)

Franciscan church

Old city hall

St. Martins cathedral

Slovakian National gallery

Nivy

Dunaj →

37

Bratislava to Komárno (SK)

106.5 km

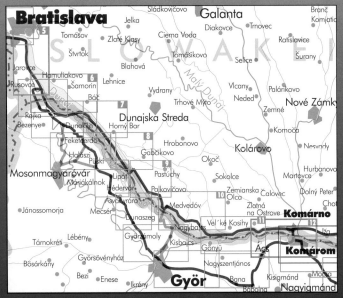

Construction of the hydro-electric power plant on the Danube turned this part of the river into a large reservoir and destroyed major portions of a previously undisturbed natural landscape. The man-made canal extends as far as Medved'ov. At Klížka Nemá the Mosoni Duna from Hungary converges with the main Danube. Because the infrastructure for tourists between Bratislava and Komárno is not yet well-developed, we recommend planning this stage of the trip carefully.

Many kilometers of straight, paved roads along the crowns of the man-made dikes along the Danube are open to cyclists and other recreation-seekers. Your route follows the right side of the reservoir to Gabíkovo. After Gabíkovo parts of the route switch to quiet country roads until one comes to southern Slovakia and the town of Komárno.

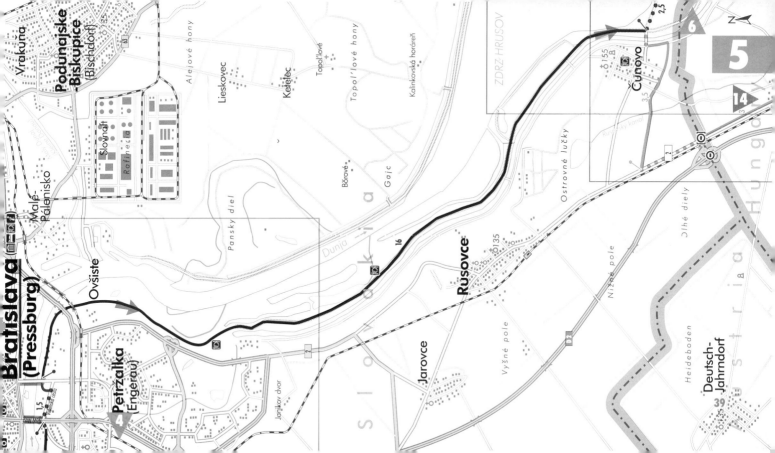

Bratislava to Gabikovo
along the right bank **52 km**

Tip: Downstream from Bratislava one can ride on either side of the dammed Danube, but the last section on the left side is closed to the public. For this reason we recommend taking the right side, which is the route described in these pages.

Just before the Nový Most bridge the main route goes through a barrier ~ turn left here ~ and proceed next to a moderately busy street ~ a short distance before the next main right-of-way street turn left towards the Danube ~ there is a prominent tower here ~ follow the road toward the right ~ go under the bridge ~ a short distance past the bridge look for painted markings on the road surface pointing the way left and up to the dam ~ ride along the dam ~ proceed for some time next to busy roads ~ until the roads veer away from the dike~ ride past an industrial area ~ the main route continues along the dike ~ past a rest area ~ the path on the dike runs

Dike near Čunovo

parallel to a small road that runs along the base of the dam on the right side ~ continue along the dike until you reach an intersection near Čunovo.

Čunovo

Danubiana Meulensteen Art Museum,
✆ 2/62528501, Open: May-Oct. Tues-Sun 10-20, Oct-May Tues-Sun 10-18. The museum in the middle of a park filled with futuristic sculptures was opened in 2000. On display are works from artists' private collections as well as the Meulensteen Foundation collection.

Stay left at this intersection ~ cross the dike, at the end of which the Danubiana Meulensteen Art Museum is located ~ continue along the dike between the reservoir and the Danube past the towns of Dobrohošt' and Vojka.

Tip: At Vojka one can take a ferry across the reservoir to Kyselica. The next possibility to cross to the left bank is at Gabíkovo.

The Gabčíkovo dam

Planning and construction of the huge Gabčíkovo-Nagymaros hydro-electric project on the Danube began during communist rule in Hungary and Czechoslovakia. After the revolutions of 1989, opposition to the project grew among environmentalists and people living along the river, who said the dam and the huge man-made reservoir would destroy a sensitive and unique ecosystem between Dunakiliti on the Hungarian side and Palkovicovo on the Slovak side. Hungary withdrew from the project, but Slovakia pushed ahead and in 1992 diverted most of the river's water into the new reservoir.

The project consists of three dams, the first of which is a barrage on Hungarian terri-

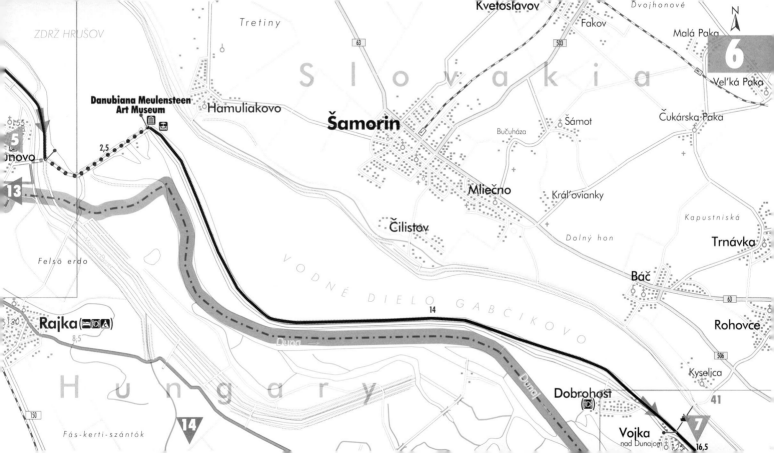

ZDRŽ HRUŠOV

Tretiny

Kvetoslavov

Dvojhonové

Fakov

Malá Paka

63

503

S l o v a k i a

Veľká Paka

6

Danubiana Meulensteen Art Museum

Hamuliakovo

Šamorin

Šámot

Čukárska Paka

Bučuháza

1,55

2,5

5

Mliečno

Kráľovianky

Kapustniská

13

Čilistov

Trnávka

Dolný hon

Báč

Rohovce

Felsö erdo

V O D N É   D I E L O   G A B Č I K O V O

63

14

Duna

1,30

Rajka

506

8,5

Duna

Kyselica

H u n g a r y

Dobrohošť

41

150

Vojka

7

Fás-kerti-szántók

14

nad Dunajom

1,25

16,5

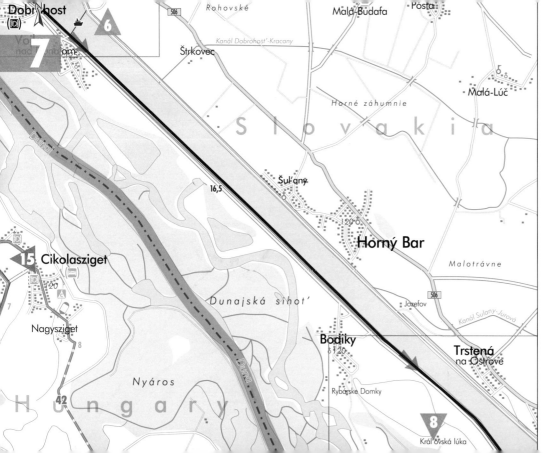

tory. It channels up to 97.5 percent of the Danube's waters into the man-made reservoir formed by two 17-kilometer dikes that are up to 18 meters high and lead to the main dam across the river near the Slovak town of Gabčíkovo. A total of 150 million cubic meters of fill material were moved in the course of the project and about 4,600 hectares of flood-plain woods and meadows were flooded.

The power station at Gabčíkovo has eight turbines. Twice a day the sluices are opened to feed the turbines and satisfy peak power demand.

A busy road crosses the locks.

Tip: Continue straight to reach Gabčíkovo, a small town with overnight accommodations and restaurants.

Gabčíkovo

Phone area code: 0709

✠ Kirche. Built in the 14th century, modified in the 18th century. The largest church in the region.

✼ Renaissance palace with 17th century gardens.

Gabčíkovo to Medved'ov   **12.5 km**

Turn right at the first opportunity after the locks ⌇ the right turn in very sharp ⌇ then straight to the dike ⌇ and continue along the left bank on the road on the dike past the town of Sap – which has an inn where one can find refreshments – and on towards Medved'ov.

Medved'ov

❌ Border crossing to Hungary (Vámosszabadi), open 24 hours a day

On the Hungarian side to Györ   **21 km**

Take the regular road across the border into Hungary ⌇ turn left when you reach the point where bicycles are not allowed ⌇ make the sharp turn back towards Slovakia ⌇ and then onto the dike ⌇ the road on the dike comes to an unpaved road ⌇ turn right here ⌇ towards **Vámosszabadi** ⌇ then left towards **Nagybajcs** ⌇ in the village turn

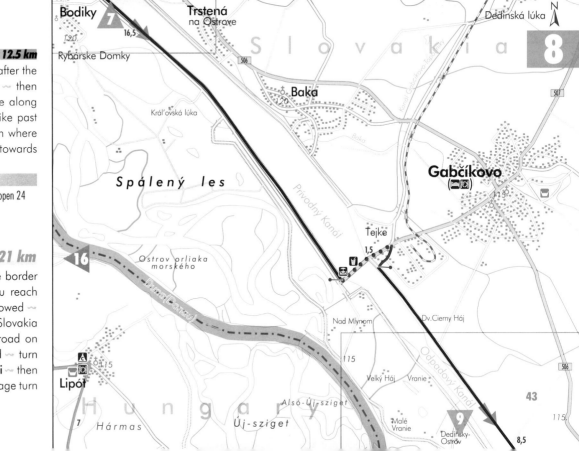

43

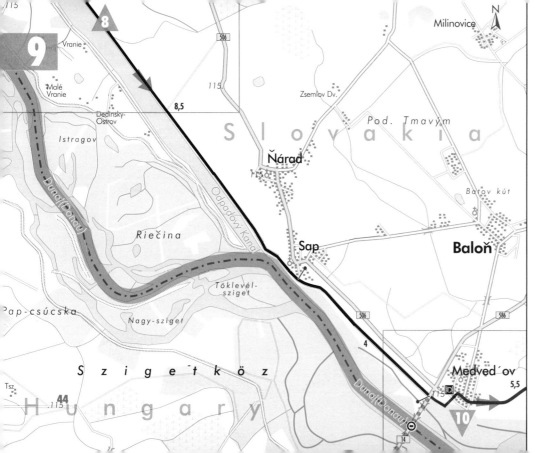

9

8

Vranie

Malé
Vranie

Dedinsky-
Ostrov

Istragov

115.

8,5

Dunaj(Donau)

Riečina

Odpadový kanál

S l o v a k i a

Milinovice

506

115.

Zsemlov Dv.

Pod. Tmavým

Ňárad

115.

Baťov kút

Sap

Baloň

Pap-csúcska

*Töklevél-
sziget*

Nagy-sziget

506

586

4

S z i g e t k ö z

Tsz.

.115

44

H u n g a r y

Dunaj(Donau)

Medved´ov

5,5

115.

14

10

right at the inn, towards **Kisbajcs** ～ and proceed about 2.5 kilometers to the outskirts of Györ ～ stay on this road and ride into the center ～ cross the larger street and proceed to the Small Danube.

Tip: Here you join the main Danube Cycle Route on the Hungarian side of the river. The description of the route and maps start on page 63, map 19 (Györ).

Medved'ov to Velké Kosihy · 22.5 km

Cross the E 575 ～ and go straight on a narrow street ～ turn left at the first opportunity

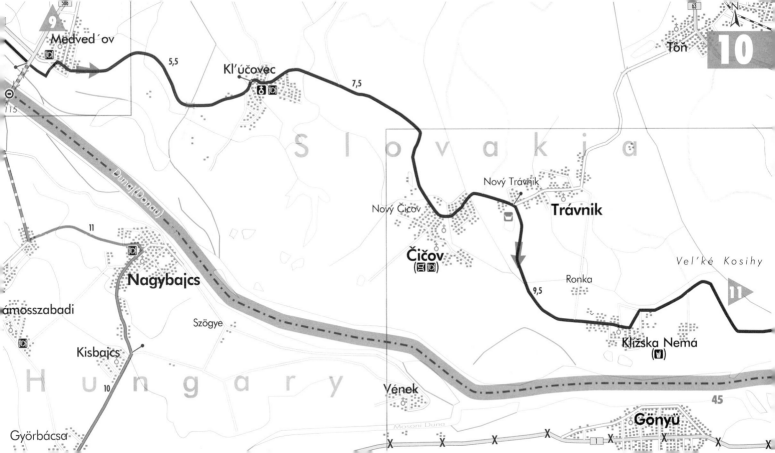

and ride into Medved'ov ∿ stay right and cycle on to **Klúčovec** and **Číčov**.

Tip: From this point the ride on the Slovak side of the river leaves the dikes along the river and follows old country lanes lined with shade trees.

The countryside between Medved'ov and Klúovec is especially pretty. Most of the creeks and canals here are lined with ancient willows, from which the local residents harvest rods in winter and which sustain an active tradition in basket-making. The route also passes directly by a number of inviting lakes, for example in Číčov or in Klížska Nemá, where sweaty cyclists can go for a refreshing swim on hot summers days.

Klúčovec

🅱 **Town church** with an onion-top steeple, which is not common in this region. If you wish to view the church, bear in mind that most churches in Slovakia are often closed. Opening times are usually posted at the entrance, and you can be sure churches are open before and after church services.

Follow the main road through Číčov ∿ a short distance before Trávnik turn right towards **Klížska Nemá**.

46

Klížska Nemá

In five kilometers you reach the town of **Velké Kosihy**.

Velké Kosihy

Tip: Between Velké Kosihy and Komárno the route follows about 17.5 kilometers of unpaved roads on the main dike next to the river. There are several gates that may pose problems for cyclists towing trailers. As an alternative, ride from Velké Kosihy to Okánikovo and then take the No. 63 state road towards Komárno.

Velké Kosihy to Komárno   *19.5 km*

Right after the edge of town turn right on the first street ∿ then straight ∿ all the way to the river flood barrier ∿ when you reach the river, continue along the dam.

The next few kilometers take you through a nature reserve that was once home to a population of european bustards. They were rare even before the power station was completed, and are now almost completely gone. There are, nevertheless, other birds, including grey herons.

Pass the village of **Zlatná Na Ostrove** as you ride along the dike. There is a dilapidated palace here, and a campground ∿ continue to **Nová Stráž** and on towards Komárno ∿ ride under the railroad bridge ∿ and then back up to the crown of the embankment ∿ after about 200 meters turn left away from the road on the top of the embankment ∿ and stay to the right ∿ you are now on a peninsula ∿ ride down a handsome avenue lined with sycamores, past a guest house and restaurants ∿ and directly to the border station ∿ turn left to reach the center of Komárno.

Komárno

Postal code: 94501; Phone area code: 035

ℹ **Tourist information**, Zupná c. 5, ✆ 7730063, www.komarno.sk

🏛 **Museum of Hungarian and Danube culture**, Nádor u. 13, ✆ 7731476, Open: Tues-Sat 9-17. Archaeological artifacts, folklore and history, plus 18th and 19th century paintings.

🏛 **Zichy Palast**, Klapka György Pl. 9, Open: Tues-Sat 9-17. Historic exhibition. The Hungarian writer Jókai (1825-1904) and Franz Lehár Sohn are two famous sons of the city.

🅱 **Andreas church** (18th century)

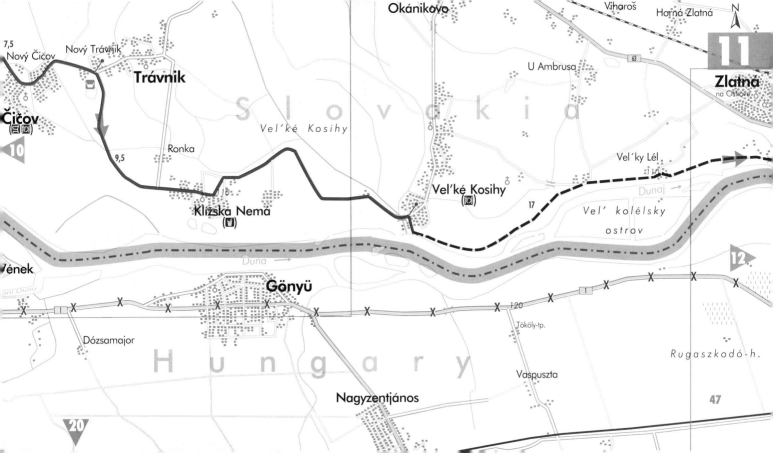

Okánikovo

Viharoš

Horná Zlatná

N

7,5
Nový Čičov

Nový Trávnik

Trávnik

U Ambrusa

63

11

Zlatná
na Ostrove

Čičov
(⊟|◎)

Slovakia

Vel'ké Kosihy

10

Ronka

9,5

Vel'ky Lél

Vel'ké Kosihy
(◎)

17

Vel´ky Lél

110

10

Klížska Nema
(♨)

Dunaj →

Vel' kolélsky

ostrov

12

Duna →

Vének

Gönyü

1

X   X   X   X

X

X   120

X   X   X   X   X

1

Dózsamajor

Tököly-tp.

Rugaszkodó-h.

Hungary

Vaspuszta

47

Nagyzentjános

20

- ⓪ **Old and new castle,** ☎ 907178906. At the west end of the new fortress stands the inscription, "nec arte nec marte" ("not by cunning nor by force") – appropriate words for what looks like an almost impregnable fortification.
- ✴ **Fortifications.** The 16th century renaissance fortress, built to defend against the Turks, and the new fortress from the late 17th century, were the two largest of their kind in the kingdom.
- ✴ **Europa Square:** complex of 45 buildings representing the individual nations of Europe, constructed 1999/2000 under the direction of the architects Litomericzky and Varga.
- ✴ **Border crossing to Komárno,** open 24 hours

Komárno is the Slovak half of a city that once occupied both sides of the river. After World War I, when European maps were redrawn, the Danube became the border between Hungary and Czechoslovakia. The city on the Hungarian side of the river is today called Komárom.

In the late Stone Age, small settlements formed in the area where the Vah meets the Danube. Later the Romans arrived and built the Clementia military camp. In the 16th century, a Renaissance fortress was built to protect the area from the Turks. It and the new fortress were

among the largest the monarchy held. Today it is regarded a national memorial.

The Podunajské Museum (Danube region museum) contains archaeological artifacts from Roman times as well as other items documenting the history, folklore, biology and art of the region. The composer Franz Lehár and the Hungarian writer Mór Jókai were both born in Komárno.

Today Komárno is a growing industrial town and an important center of Slovakia's shipbuilding industry. The city's large shipyards produce vessels that ply the Danube as well as ocean-going ships.

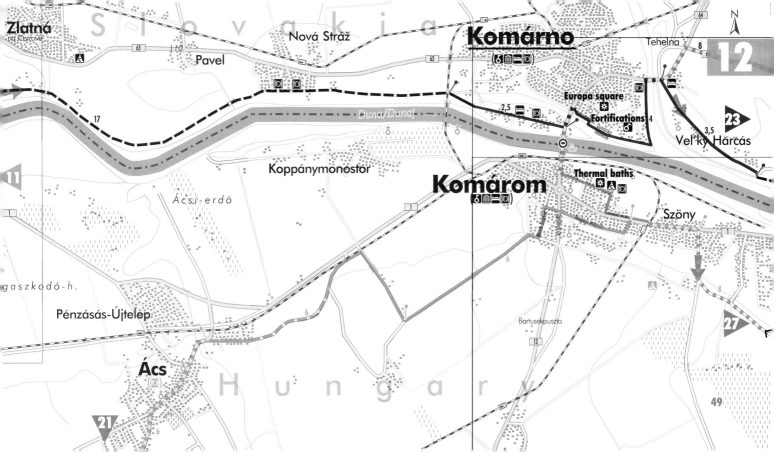

Bratislava to Komárom (H)

135 km

It is a short distance from Bratislava to the Hungarian border at Rajka. The route crosses the "Szigetköz" – a large wetlands area bounded by the Danube and the Mosoni Duna (Small Danube). In many of the smaller villages one can still find straw-covered farmhouses. Discover Mosonmagyaróvár, the charming old "city of 17 bridges", or the provincial capital Györ with its many sights. Horse-lovers will enjoy the Bábolna stables, and the thermal baths at Komárom offer relaxation and restorative waters.

The flat landscape between Bratislava and Györ is outstanding for bicycle riding. The paved country road leads through a landscape of quiet old Hungarian villages. Between Hédervár and Györ the route mostly follows a bicycle path. After Györ you will leave the Mosoni Duna and ride through a gently rolling landscape to Komárom.

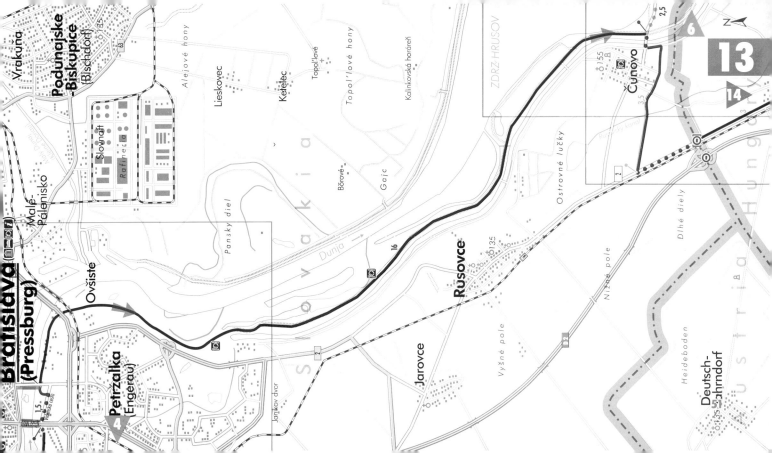

Bratislava to Čunovo 17.5 km

Tip: From Bratislava to Čunovo, follow the route description on page 40, where the first stage of the Slovak route goes down the Hungarian side of the river.

Čunovo to Rajka 6.5 km

Turn right down from the causeway just before the dam at Čunovo ∾ follow the road ∾ which takes you south of Čunovo (Sarndorf) in a long loop around the town.

Čunovo

Tip: Čunovo has a fine little inn where one can sit on an outdoor terrace and enjoy a Slovakian beer (pivo). There is also a pizzeria.

Turn left on the main national road with traffic headed for the Hungarian border.

Tip: For motorized traffic, the border crossing is open only to Hungarian and Slovak citizens. Any bicyclist with a valid passport will also be permitted to pass.

A wall runs along the road that leads out of the village ∾ at the end of the wall turn right ∾ cross

Little Danube in Hungary

a small bridge ∾ and turn left on the main national road with traffic headed for the Hungarian border ∾ just past the passport check turn onto the bicycle path that runs alongside the main road ∾ after 1.5 kilometers enter Rajka.

Rajka

Rajka to Dunakiliti 8.5 km

The bicycle path goes as far as Rajka ∾ at the third junction turn left away from the main road ∾ proceed straight into the village to the first fork in the road ∾ turn right ∾ at the edge of town turn right at the traffic island. The next destination is Dunakiliti ∾ take the quiet country

lane across the **Mosoni Duna** (Little Danube).

The Little Danube is actually just a branch of the river. Both currents flow around the Szigetköz island.

Szigetköz

Szigetköz means "thousand islands" and refers to the wetlands that runs along the Danube between Rajka and Györ. The area is bounded by the Danube, or Duna in Hungarian, to the north and the Little Danube, or Mosoni Duna, to the south.

After breaking through the mountains at Bratislava, the Danube forms a delta as it spreads into the Small Hungarian Plain. This flood plain makes the Austrian March plains seem small in comparison. North of Rajka one stream, the Mosoni Danu, branches southward from the main river. It winds its way slowly through many villages and towns like Dunakiliti and Feketeerdö on its way to Györ.

At Mosonmagyaróvár the Mosoni Duna converges with the Leitha. In Györ the stream is joined by the Rábca and the Rába before it returns to the main Danube at Vének. The flat and fertile lands of the Szigetköz covered with grain, pastures and sunflowers. At harvest the huge piles of straw seem to be the tallest objects in sight. The Szigetköz – a quiet and pleasant landscape ideal for relaxed bicycle touring.

Take the quiet country lane to Dunakiliti.

Tip: In Dunakiliti the bicycle tourist faces a decision: either follow the main route, which leaves the Danube and heads to the interesting small city of Mosonmagyaróvár, or stay close to the river and proceed from one small village to the next, with stretches on the unpaved causeway. The two routes meet again after Püski.

Dunakiliti

Tip: From the church, the alternative route continues almost straight ahead via Feketeerdö to Mosonmagyaróvár. The route is shown on Maps 15 and 16. If you wish to stay on the main route along the Danube, turn left towards Halászi or Tejfalusziget.

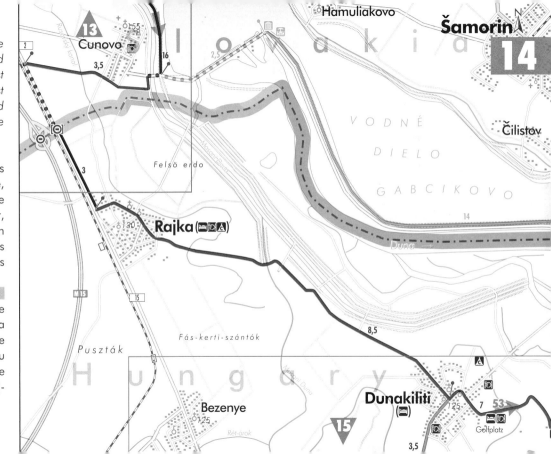

Tip: The main route continues almost straight from the church towards Feketeerdö and Mosonmagyaróvár. If you wish to stay close to the river turn left towards Tejfalusziget.

Alternate route Dunakiliti to Püski via Mosonmagyaróvár   21 km

In Dunakiliti turn right at the church ～ the next town is **Feketeerdö**.

Follow the country road towards the small city of **Mosonmagyaróvár** ～ stay left at the intersection with **Halászi utca**.

Tip: Turn right at this intersection to enter the center of the city.

Mosonmagyaróvár

Postal code: 9200; Phone area code: 96

🛈 **Tourinform**, Kápclna tér 16, ✆ 206304

🛈 **Ciklámen Tourist**, Fö út 8., ✆ 217344

🏛 **Hanság Museum**, Szent István u. 1, ✆ 213834, Open: May-Sept, Tues-Sun 10-18, Oct-April, 10-16. Museum with archaeological, historic and ethno-graphic collections about the nearby Hanság national park, a nature reserve.

🏛 **Cselley Haus**, Fö u. 19, ✆ 212094, Open: May-Sept, Tues-Sun 10-18, Oct-April, Tues-Sun 12-16.

🏰 **Burg Óvár**, on the Leitha Island. Built in the 13th century. Today an agricultural institute. The tunnel vault of the entrance has four Gothic sitting niches (15th century). Also surviving are two towers, the moats, casemates, prison cells and outer walls.

🏰 **Old Church**, St. László tér. With grave monument to the Archduke Friedrich and Archduchess Isabella.

❇ **Lucsony utca** (Lucsony Street). A row of old houses built in a provincial baroque style.

🌊 **Thermal spa**, Kolbai K. u. 10, ✆ 204411 or 211533, Open: Mon 8-18, Tues-Fri 8-20, Sat, Sun 8-19.

The "gate of Hungary," as the oldest city in the district is known, was first settled by the Romans in the first century before Christ. It attained its current form in 1939, when the neighboring towns of Moson and Magyaróvár were united, creating today's tongue-twister name.

The old city center is noteworthy for its collection of baroque buildings. The river Leitha (Hungarian Lajta) curves through the center before it converges with the Mosoni Duna. The one-time swamplands were drained with numerous irrigation canals, which today contribute to the city's charm. A total of 17 bridges cross these various streams.

The city's well-preserved castle, Burg Óvár, with its massive defensive walls and extensive system of moats today lies in the middle of a park. When one enters the castle through the main gate, one passes several Gothic seating niches.

Today the castle and part of the city center are historic landmarks and have been exquisitely restored. A generously laid-out pedestrian area is being installed in parts of the center and along the Magyar utca. The low buildings give the town a very hospitable atmosphere, which is reinforced by the many outdoor restaurants and gardens along the street. In the middle of Malom utca (Mill Street) one can find Szent László tér with a small church. There is a bicycle path along the entire Malom utca.

The Hanság Museum, which was established in 1913, has interesting collections about local archaeology, history and ethnography.

Depart **Mosonmagyaróvár** on the bicycle path that runs along **Halászi utca** ～ proceed to **Halászi** 4.5 kilometers away.

Halászi

Ride past the church ~ after the ice-cream shop turn right towards Györ ~ 300 meters later turn left towards Püski ~ just before Püski pass an old, grown-over cemetery on the left side.

Tip: Here in Püski you can rejoin the main route to Hedervar.

Dunakiliti to Hedervár   25.5 km

Follow the main street out of Dunakiliti ~ past the athletics fields ~ after one-and-a-half kilometers enter the tiny village of **Tejfalusziget** ~ past the grass-roofed farmhouse on the left and the small church ~ and down an ancient tree-lined avenue to towards the next village ~ the road turns to the right, exactly in the curve there is an unpaved track that goes straight towards the dike.

Tip: This is the first opportunity to switch to the rough gravel track on top of the dike. You cannot ride fast, but the track stays close to the Danube and its lush flood-plains.

Take the paved country road towards **Doborgazsziget**, a neighborhood of Dunasziget ~ straight ahead.

Dunasziget

Tip: In Dunasziget you can again choose between two alternatives. Either follow the signs and take the main route via Cikolasziget to Püski, or ride through Halászi to Püski, if you prefer asphalt roads and wish to avoid the unpaved stretch between Cikolasziget and Püski.

Alternate route
via Halaszi   14.5 km

If you selected the option via Halászi, then turn left in **Dunasziget** towards Halászi~ a short distance later cross a bridge and stay on this road~ ride past the turn-off to Cikolasziget ~ and continue along the country road to **Halászi** ~ stay left in the curve before you reach the main road ~300 meters later turn left towards Püski ~ just before Püski pass an old, grown-over cemetery on the left side.

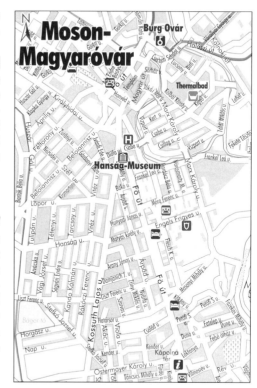

Püski

At the church in Püski you have the option of turning left and joining the main route, or you can take the road that curves to the right and ride through the village and continue on to **Dunaremete** ~ this option rejoins the main route just before Dunaremete.

If you wish to follow the main route, first turn left in Dunasziget towards Halaszi and then follow the road ~ before it reaches the bridge ~ turn left in the road that branches off towards Cikolasziget ~ stay on the country road in the next town.

Cikolasziget

Follow the main road through the village ~ the road curves to the right ~ keep going on this road ~ the main road makes an "S", first you turn left, then right ~ at the fork at the end of town stay right ~ and proceed straight 56 ~ at the end of the town go left ~ and follow the bicycle sign towards Püski and Györ ~ the next section is unpaved ~ and then becomes a paved, but somewhat rough, road that leads into Püski.

Püski

At the edge of Püski turn left at the intersection with the sign towards Kisbodak.

To the left to leave Püski ~ ride less than one kilometer and enter **Kisbodak** ~ straight ahead ~ on the left there is a cemetery ~ continue straight to a small traffic circle ~ turn right, away from the circle ~ and come to a fork in the road where a cross stands ~ stay right at this fork ~ at the end of the village cross a small bridge ~ ride straight towards the flood-plain forest ~ onto an unpaved track ~ and turn right and ride along the woods ~ after about one kilometer turn right and towards the road that leads from Püski to **Dunaremete**. Turn left and continue along the country lane

to **Lipót.**

Lipót

As you enter town there is a rest area on the left ~ continue to the main road ~ and turn left there ~ there is a small bicycle sign ~ follow the course of the road to the church ~ stay right here ~ look for the sign to Hérdervár.

In Lipot turn right towards Hédervár some 3.5 kilometers away.

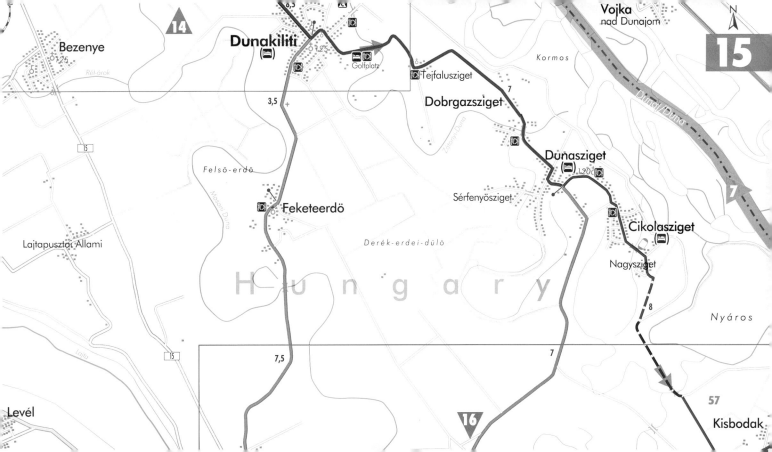

Hédervár

⑥ Hédervár castle. Large castle, originally Gothic, later expanded in the renaissance style, now stands in the middle of a protected parkland. According to local legend, the massive oak tree in front of the Gothic chapel is at least 1,000 years old. The castle is in private hands and has been converted to a hotel.

The recently renovated Hédervár castle, a magnificent fortified palace that grew out of a medieval fortress, stands in the middle of a fine park. The entrance is guarded by two stone lions. The castle has been refurbished as a hotel that opened in January 2004. Diagonally across from the church stands a small straw-roofed house. The straw roofs of the region were not only cute to look at, but said to be more weather resistant than shingled roofs.

Hédervar to Györ   26 km

Tip: Do not be confused by the sign indicating a spa. Hédervár does not have a spa – the sign refers to the baths in Lipót.

As you enter town turn left on the main road ∿ take the main street straight through town ∿ towards Àsványráró ∿ as you leave town pick

Dunasziget

up the paved bicycle lane on the right side

Starting in the town there is a bicycle lane on the roadway ∿ as you leave town the bicycle path runs parallel to the road ∿ and separated by a small green strip ∿ this bicycle path continues all the way to Gyor ∿ the route to Györ goes past an old church ∿ and reaches Asványráró after 3 kilometers.

Àsványráró

The fishery is the oldest surviving industry in this town, where other trades like towing ships, milling grain, and washing gold have all disappeared. The last gold-panner in Asványráró died in 1944. Some hobbyists still try their luck panning for gold, however, with modest success.

Entering town there is a cycling lane on the side of the road ∿ turn right at the traffic circle at the church ∿ and follow the sign towards Györ

The street through town has a bicycle lane. At the edge of the community a paved bicycle path starts next to the road ∿ it is paved for the entire 7 kilometers to Dunaszeg.

Dunaszeg

Tip: Here you have two alternative routes for reaching Györ: Continue on the bicycle path next to the country road to Györ or take the idyllic 12.5 kilometer causeway along the Mosoni Duna (Little Danube).

The unpaved track next to the river is quieter and prettier. However, it can only be recommended for riders and bicycles prepared to deal with a sometimes-rough surface.

Alternative route along the Mosoni Duna   12.5 km

To reach the Mosoni Duna, in Dunaszeg 200 meters past the curve at the supermarket turn right on **Kossuth Lajos** ∿ the street is not hard to find. Look for the blue street sign. ∿ When

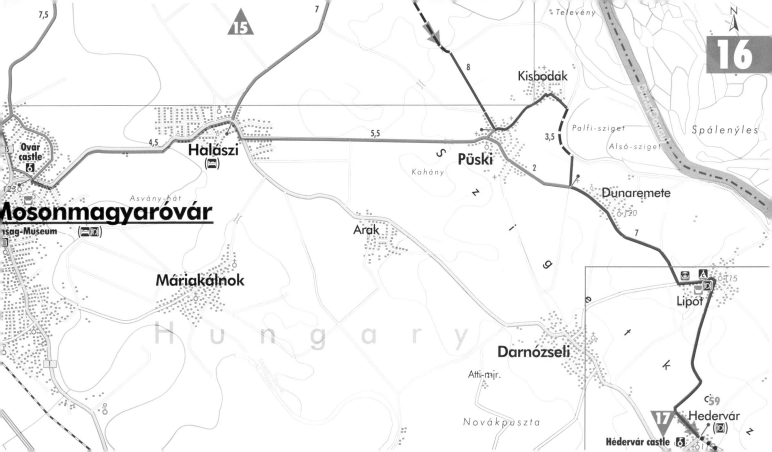

7,5

15

7

Televény

16

8

Kisbodak

Ovár castle

Palfi-sziget

Spálenýles

15

4,5

Halászi

5,5

3,5

Alsó-sziget

125

Püski

2

Kohány

Dunaremete

Mosonmagyaróvár

Ásvány-hát

120

ság-Museum

7

Arak

Máriakálnok

115

Lipót

H u n g a r y

e

Darnózseli

Atti-mjr.

59

17

Hedervár

Novákpuszta

Hédervár castle

115

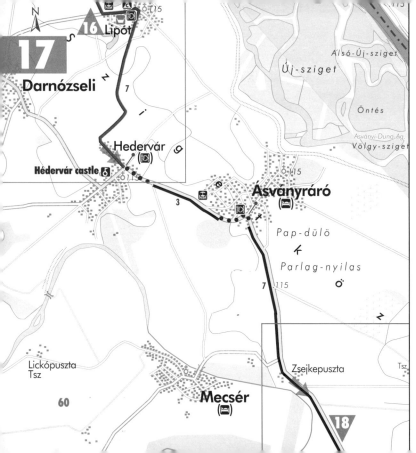

17

Darnózseli

16 Lipót

7

Hédervár

Hédervár castle

Ásványráró

Új-sziget

Alsó-Új-sziget

Öntés

Ásványi-Dung-Ág.
Völgy-sziget

Pap-dülö

Parlag-nyilas

7 115

Lickópuszta
Tsz

Zsejkepuszta

Tsz

Mecsér

18

Hédervár castle

you reach the causeway turn left towards Györ ﹏ to the right is a broad and idyllic flood plain ﹏ after about 10 kilometers the track reaches a fork ﹏ straight ahead leads back to the main road, or turn right on the bicycle trail into Györ.

If in Dunaszeg you stay on the main route, on the bicycle trail next to the road, you ride through the villages of Györladamér, Györzámoly﹏ and then come to the village of Györújfalu ﹏ near the end of the village come to a square with two small churches ﹏ turn right a short distance past the church ﹏ and go diagonally across the square ﹏ and to the right next to a restaurant into a small street

Tip: The cycling route here is marked with a small blue sign.

After a short distance the bicycle path meets with the road to Györ ﹏ before finally reaching the Györ city boundary.

Tip: It is important to turn right at the sign pointing to the center of town. Not doing so lands the bicyclist on the main national road to Vámoszsabadi, which is no fun at all.

Győr, basilica

Continue straight ahead on **Héderváry ut.** the bicycle path switches to the left side of the street ～ at the next intersection follow the main road ～ cross to the other side of the street ～ on the bicycle path next to the street to **Kossuth híd,** an imposing steel bridge.

Tip: From the bridge one can look to the right to see the grounds of the thermal baths on the "Sziget". A bronze figure stands at the tip of the island. This is also a good place to start a tour of the city, which one can ride by bicycle.

Győr

Postal code: 9021; Phone area code: 096

🛈 **Tourinform Győr,** Árpád u. 32, ✆ 311771.

🏛 **Janus Xantus Museum,** Széchenyi tér 5, ✆ 310588, Open: May-Oct, Mon-Sun 10-18, Nov-April, Mon-Sun 10-14. Ethnology collections dedicated to Hungarian naturalist and explorer Janus Xantus (1825-1894) on display in a house dating from 1741-43.

🏛 **Imre Patkó Collection,** Széchenyi tér 4, ✆ 310588, Open: April-Oct, Tues-Sun 10-18. Early baroque Eisenklotz House (17th century) contains Hungarian and European artworks of the 20th century, Asian arts and crafts from the 18th to 20th centuries, and an ethnographic collection from Africa.

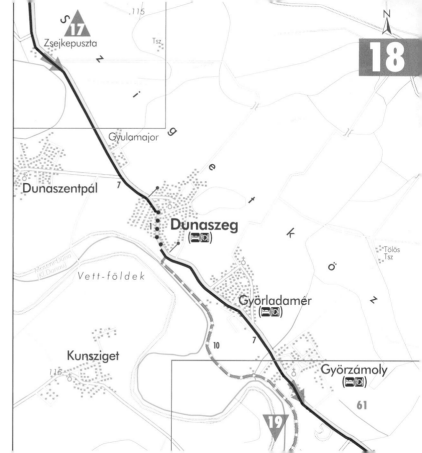

Györ, city hall

🏛 **Györ National Theater**, Czuczor Gergely u. The facade decoration on the modern theatre building was done by Victor Vasarely, a Hungarian painter born in 1908. Home of one of the best dance ensembles in central Europe, the Györ Ballet.

🏛 **Basilica**, Káptalandomb. Only the apse remains of the original 13th century Gothic church. The classical facade dates to 1823. The interior altars and frescos were done by Franz Anton Maulbertsch (1724-96).

🏛 **Benedictine church**, Széchenyi tér. Built 1635-41 according to plans by Baccio del Biancho.

🏛 **Carmelite church**, Bécsi kapu tér. Baroque facade and interior of the church (1721-25) by Martin Witwer.

🏛 **Bishops castle**, Káptalandomb. The former bishops castle with its old residential tower dates to the 12th century.

❎ **Margit Kovács exhibition**, Apáca u. 1, ☎ 326739, Open: March-Oct, Tues-Sun 10-18, Nov-Feb, Tues-Sun 10-17. Works by the ceramics artist Margit Kovács (1902-77) can be seen in the Kreszta house.

🏊 **Indoor swimming pool**, Orsszágút u. 4, ☎ 326566, Open: Mon-Sat 9-18.

💆 **Health spa**, Fürdö Tér 1, ☎ 514900, Jan-Dec, Mon-Sun 7-23

✉ **Püspök erdö**, on the Holt Duna, on the Mosuni Duna, nudist beach

🏨 **Álmos vezér**, Corvin u. 44, ☎ 335567

Györ is one of the largest and most important cities in northwestern Hungary. It lies at the confluence of the Mosoni Duna, the Rábca and the Rába rivers, which then empty into the Danube. The city's origins were in the Bronze Age. Today Györ is an important industrial city. It gained its economic importance with the Danube river port built in the 18th century.

The Celts were the first to settle in this fertile area. In the first century AD, the Romans built a town they called Arrabona. It became one of the most important border fortifications of Pannonia province. Hungarians began moving into the area at the end of the 9th century. Györ was almost completely destroyed on two occasions: once by the Turks, a second time in WWII when aerial bombardment reduced a quarter of the baroque city to ash and ruin.

When one crosses the Mosoni Duna on the Kossuth híd, one faces the old historic center of Györ. An expansive pedestrian area has been set up in the city to keep the automotive traffic at bay.

Jedlik Anyos út leads down to Széchenyi tér, an imposing square dominated by a Benedictine church with two towers. In the middle of the square stands the Maria's column. Hungary's most modern theatre building, the Györ National Theatre, resembles a ski jump and stands nearby. The facades with their black and white tiles and geometric forms were done by the world-famous Hungarian painter, Victor Vasarely. Take Arany János út to reach the flower market and the Raab River. The Carmelite church on Bécsi kapu tér, the Vienna Gate Square, was built between 1721 and 1725. The magnificent baroque facade is done up in a powerful yellow tone. Rising above

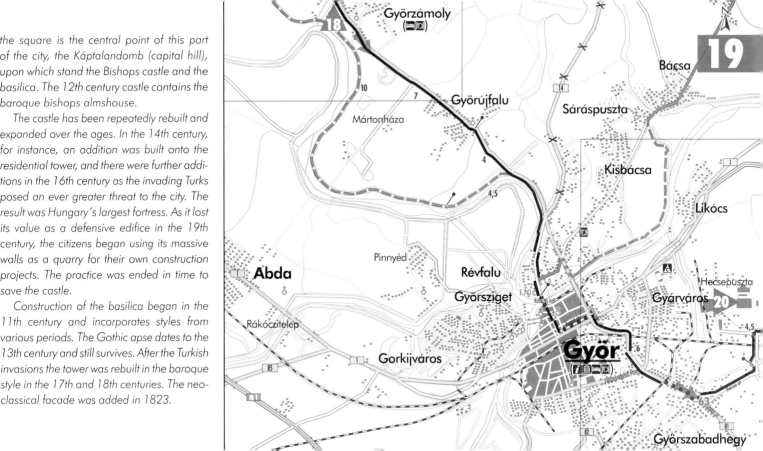

the square is the central point of this part of the city, the Káptalandomb (capital hill), upon which stand the Bishops castle and the basilica. The 12th century castle contains the baroque bishops almshouse.

The castle has been repeatedly rebuilt and expanded over the ages. In the 14th century, for instance, an addition was built onto the residential tower, and there were further additions in the 16th century as the invading Turks posed an ever greater threat to the city. The result was Hungary's largest fortress. As it lost its value as a defensive edifice in the 19th century, the citizens began using its massive walls as a quarry for their own construction projects. The practice was ended in time to save the castle.

Construction of the basilica began in the 11th century and incorporates styles from various periods. The Gothic apse dates to the 13th century and still survives. After the Turkish invasions the tower was rebuilt in the baroque style in the 17th and 18th centuries. The neoclassical facade was added in 1823.

The Ladislaus chapel was completed in 1404. It contains the Hermes, a gold-plated silver bust holding the skull of King Ladislaus the holy.

Visitors who wish to learn more about these stories and the city's history may wish to visit "János Xantus Museum." In addition to exhibits about Győr and the surrounding area, the museum also contains an ethnographic section. Other noteworthy buildings in the city include the city hall, the Kreszta House with its exhibits of ceramics by Margit Kovács and the Altabak house.

Győr to Bábolna   32.5 km

The next stage starts from the **Kossuth híd** in Győr~ ride straight into the city and past the Kreszta house on **Jedlik Ányos u.** ~ through the pedestrian zone~ which ends at **Kisfaludy u.** which you cross and continue straight ahead~ to **Czuczor Gergely u.** where there is a bicycle path on both sides of the street~ turn left on **Àrpád út** and follow it straight to **Fehérvári út** ~ the main road out of the city towards Tata ~ this road has heavy

Győr

traffic, and a bicycle path on the left side of the roadway.

After the railroad bridge the bicycle path switches to the other side of the road. After the intersection of **Felszabadulás útca** it continues on the right ~ the bicycle path ends after the tunnel under the railroad ~ Continue on the busy road ~ until you reach a large traffic circle ~ at the circle the bicycle path switches to the left side of the road ~ ride in a loop around the

circle ~ and leave it in the direction of Tata ~ you are now on **Hecsei ut** ~ stay on the bicycle path to the left of the main road ~ stay left ~ at the intersection turn to the left ~ and approach another traffic circle~ pass it on the left side and continue straight ahead ~ across a railroad bridge ~ until you reach an intersection ~ go straight through the intersection ~ turn right ~ turn left onto a bicycle path ~ after about 250 meters turn left into the fields ~ straight~ cross a small railroad line~ and continue straight towards **Győrszentiván~** the bicycle path ends just before the traffic circle.

Győrszentiván

At the traffic circle take the first street right out to **Egressy utca** ~ when you come to a larger, right-of-way street cross it ~ and take the street slightly to the right on the other side of the main road~ this is still **Egressy utca** ~ at the following main road turn left towards Temetö~ on the right you can see a cemetery ~ take the first right ~ and make a curve to the left and then straight parallel to the railroad~ pass the train station ~ at the next larger road go straight on

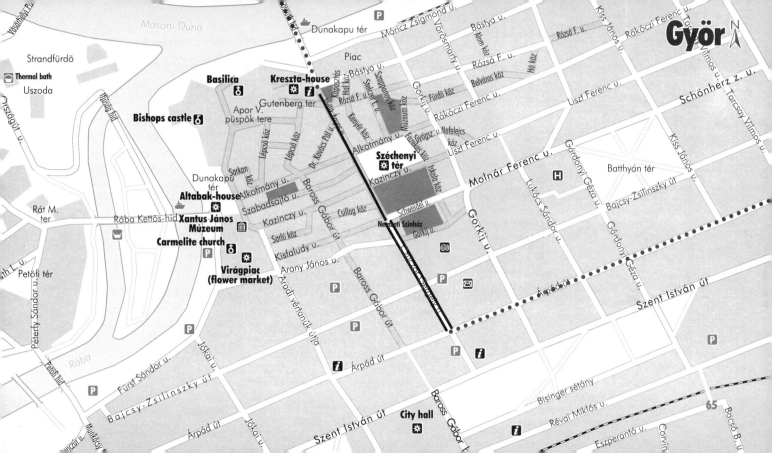

Vasut utca ~ continue straight to the railroad crossing ~ cross the tracks ~ left ~ then the first street right ~ and proceed towards **Nagyhegy**.

Nagyhegy

Proceed straight through ~ until you reach a T-intersection ~ turn left there ~ and follow this unpaved road ~ across a bridge over the motorway ~ the road on the right, past the village of **Szölöhegy** ~ continue to the intersection and keep going until you reach the main road ~ turn left on the moderately busily-traveled road to **Bönyrétalap**.

Bönyrétalap

Follow the road into **Böny** ~ then follow signs for Tata ~ and proceed to **Bana**.

Bana

Turn left just before the first church and follow the road ~ at the second church turn right towards Tata. The next destination is the small

Bábolna

city of Bábolna, which is an important stop for all equestrians ~ a bicycle path begins at the edge of town on the right side of the road and comes to an end at the next large intersection ~ turn left there, towards Acs.

Tip: We recommend a visit to the stables and the horse museum, which is located on the main street.

Bábolna

Postal code: 2943; Phone area code: 34

🏛 **Horse museum**, across from the stables, ☎ 569-111, hunting and coach museum, guide tours through the riding hall and stables. The tour takes about 90 minutes.

✱ **Bábolna Stud Farm**, Mészáros u. 1 The famous stud was established in 1789, is equipped with a magnificent interior courtyard. It is famous for its racing horses.

✱ **Horse presentations**. For a fee, horses are presented to visitors who make appointments.

Bábolna is a tidy and prosperous looking little town, thanks in part to the large agricultural cooperative that built a reputation throughout the former eastern-bloc and the far east. In the center of the town stands an old imperial building that houses Bábolna's famous stud. This is where Hungary's fastest and best racing thoroughbreds are bred and trained.

The entire town is built around the stud, which was founded in 1789. For health reasons, tourists may not visit the horses in their stables.

Across from the stud is an equestrian museum with a large collection of artworks and items related to horses and horse-riding, including richly-decorated saddles, stirrups, uniforms and, of course, pictures of fine horses and trophies won by some of the town's best racers.

Bábolna to Komárom   22 km

Depart Bábolna on the road to Ács ~ the first significant climb starts almost as soon as you leave the town ~ then downhill to the M1 motorway bridge ~ stay right ~ cross the bridge over the M1 motorway (Vienna-Budapest) ~ the pointed white church tower in Ács is visible in the distance.

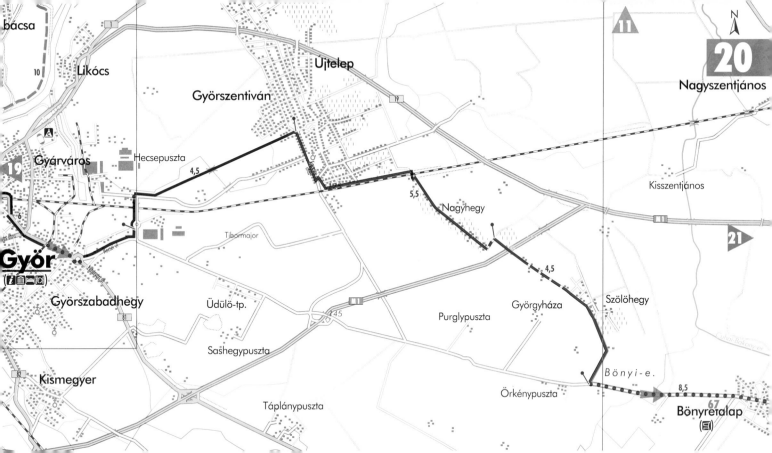

Ács

The road curves to the left as it enters Ács ~ then continue straight ~ in the center of town there is a bicycle lane along the main street, but it ends after a few hundred meters ~ the street curves to the right ~ over a small bridge ~ and then straight at the next intersection ~ and take an unpaved track into the fields ~ until you reach a small woods ~ the path runs briefly parallel to the main road ~ turn right at the next intersection ~ ignore the "no vehicles" sign and enter the paved service road ~ past two large farms ~ after the second farm turn left and continue straight towards Komárom.

At the outskirts of Komárom turn right and then immediatly left on **Marek József ut**. ~ there is a reduced speed zone posted for 40 km/h here ~ to the main road into Komárom, the heavily-used **Igmándi út**. ~ cross it and continue on **Madách Imre út** ~ continue straight ahead to a T-intersection, then left and up to the main federal road

Tip: If you turn left here and then right again, you come to the thermal baths, numerous hotels and campgrounds.

To continue on the main route follow the **B 10** to the right.

Komárom

Postal code: 2900; Phone area code: 34

🛈 **Tourinform**, Igmándi út 2, ✆ 540-590, www.komarom.hu

🏛 **Klapka György Museum**, Kelemen László u. 22, ✆ 344697, Open: 26 April-Sept Tues-Sun 10-18, Oct-25 April Tues-Sun 10-16. Frescoes and other artifacts found at Brigetio, sarcophagi with human remains, gold jewelry and items made of glass and bronze.

🏛 **Maritime Museum**, Szabadság tér 1 (town hall), ✆ 541340, Open: 26 April-Sept Tues-Sun 10-18, Oct-25 April Tues-Sun 10-16

🛡 **Fortress Igmánd** (Roman lapidarium), Igmándi eröd, ✆ 5085097, Open: 26 April-Sept 10-16, closed in the winter. Exhibits of ancient stone work, inscribed grave stones, plus sarcophagi and altar blocks.

🛡 **Fort Monostor, Monostori Eröd**, Dunapart, ✆ 540-582 Open: 15 March-Okt, Mon-Sun 9-17. The Monostor fortress is the largest modern fortification in central Europe. Built between 1850 and 1871, it consists of a complex network of fortification walls, moats and underground bunkers. Today it is maintained as a memorial to Hungary's military history.

🕍 **Roman Catholic Church**, Szent László utca. Significant example of modern Hungarian church architecture
City hall, Hösök tere. Neo-baroque town hall.

♨ **Thermal baths and campground**, Táncsics M. út 34-36, ✆ 342551. Various facilities, including six pools with water of various temperatures.

After WWI, when the border between Slovakia and Hungary was drawn, this city on the Danube was divided into the Slovak Komárno and the Hungarian Komárom. Today they are connected by the "Friendship Bridge." One important year

68

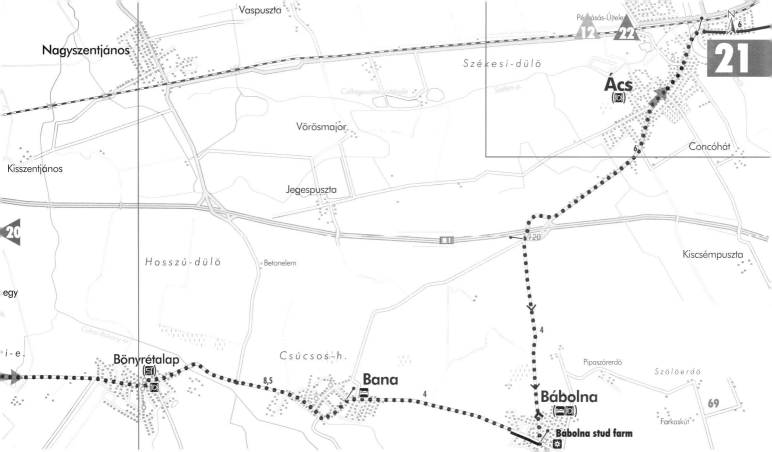

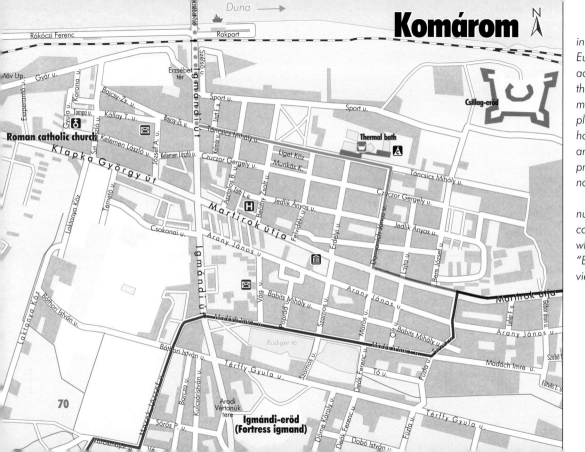

Komárom

in the city's history is 1848, the year of European revolution, when populations across the continent rebelled to demand their freedom and more say in government. The strong fortifications and supplies enabled the Habsburg troops to hold the fortress. Today the Csillag-eröd and Igmándi-eröd fortresses are still well preserved, although the first of the two is now used as a factory.

Excavations at Igmándi-eröd brought numerous objects to light, including sarcophagi and gold coins from the time when this was a Roman camp named "Brigetio". These treasures can be viewed in the museum at the site.

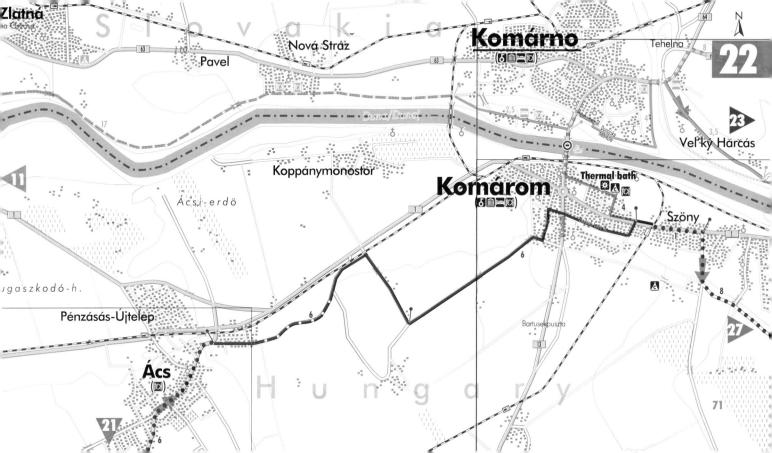

Komárno to Esztergom (SK)   55.5 km

This stage of the ride goes from Tata to Esztergom along the Slovak shore of the Danube. The cultural highlights of this stretch are Komárno, the important archaeological site at "Kelemantia," and, of course, Esztergom. Another favoured excursion destination are the two thermal-lakes at Patince. The destination and culturally most interesting piece of this stage is the city of Esztergom, the "Rome of Hungary." The huge basilica on top of a hill over the city can be seen from a great distance.

The route follows either the main national road or the often unpaved roads on the dikes along the Danube. If you prefer an alternative to the hilly stretches on the Hungarian side, this route offers an attractive alternative. It has only a few minor inclines and the landscape is similarly charming.

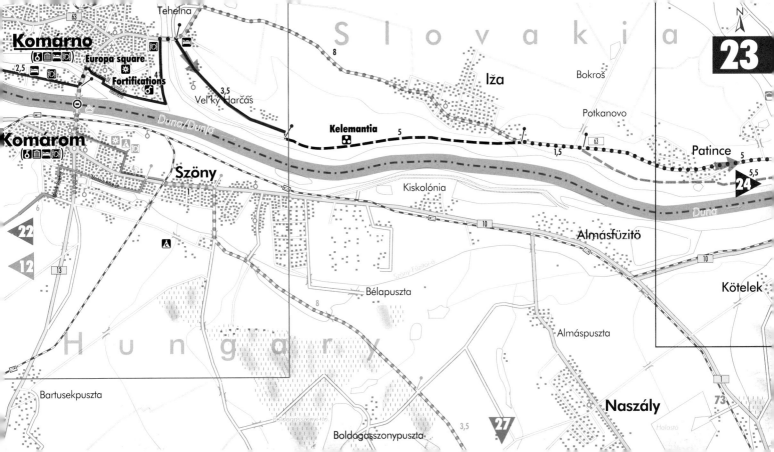

Komárno

see page 70

Postal code: 94501; Phone area code: 035

- ℹ **Tourist information,** Zupná c. 5, ☎ 7730063
- 🏛 **Danube museum** (Podunajské museum), Palatínova 13, ☎ 7731476, Open: Mon-Sun 9-17. Archaeological finds, nature and local history exhibits.
- 🏛 **Mór Jókai memorial museum,** Open: daily except Monday, 9-17. Jókai (1825-1904), Hungary's most-read novelist, came from Komárom, along with Franz Lehár.
- ♟ **Andreas church** (18th century)
- ✹ **Fortifications.** The 16th century renaissance fortress, built to defend against the Turks, and the new fortress from the late 17th century, were the two largest of their kind in the kingdom.
- ✹ **Europa Square:** complex of 45 buildings representing the individual nations of Europe, constructed 1999/2000 under the direction of the architects Litomericzky and Varga.
- ✹ **Border crossing to Komárno,** open 24 hours

Komárno to Iža   12.5 km

From the bridge across the Danube to Hungary on the right ~ turn left ~ and cross the bridge ~ at the first intersection after the bridge turn right ~ then turn right again on **Leharová**

Ul.~ turn left at the next T-intersection, into **Dunajské nebrezie** ~ and follow the course of the river through a long curve to the left ~ to just before the bridge~ turn left at the stop sign and onto the moderately-busy main road ~ and cross the bridge.

Tip: After the bridge there are two possible routes to Iza. Either take the paved No. 63 national route or ride through the village of Vel'ky Haráš and follow the dike along the Danube. This unpaved track takes you past the ruins of the old Roman military camp, "Kelemantia."

Alternate route over Iža   8 km

For this alternative route, after the bridge proceed straight on the busy road ~ before you reach the village of Tehela, turn right at the intersection and follow the moderately-busy road through Iža ~ here you can find a pharmacy and places to eat ~ follow the main road until it meets the main route.

To stay on the main route, turn right immediately after the bridge and ride along the

dike ~ go straight on the narrow country road ~ through the village of Vel'ky Haráš ~ when the main street though the village curves to the left you turn right~ and go to the dike ~ turn left on the dike track ~ and follow it past the archaeological site at Kelemantia

Kelemantia

- ✹ **Kelemantia,** a major archaeological site where a Roman military camp stood from the 2nd to the 4th centuries. The camp measured 175x175 meters and had 20 towers and four gates.

Proceed on the track to Iža ~ at the edge of the town turn right on the No. 63 main road.

Iža to Moča   12.5 km

The main cycling route and the alternate route meet here.

Tip: 1.5 kilometers after the dike and the street converge, turn right to take another alternative route on the dike.

Alternate route on the dike
south of Patince   5.5 km

Turn right away from the main road and ride along the dike next to the river ~ rejoin

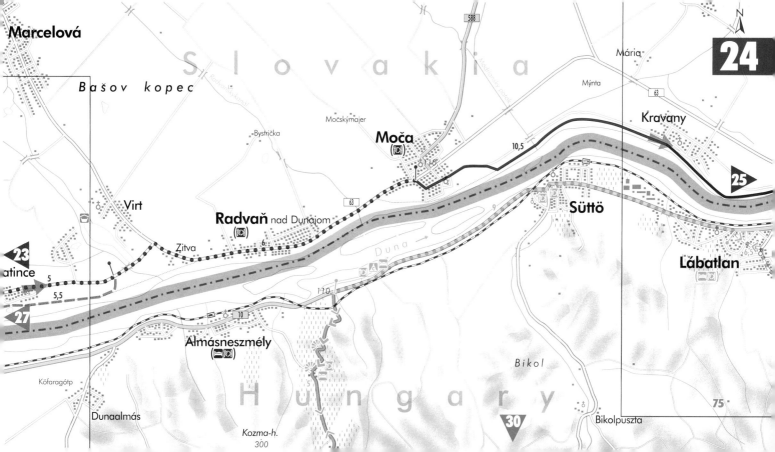

the main route at the small factory building with the chimney.

For the main route stay on the No. 63 road to Patince ∼ ride past the center of the village.

Tip: The vacation village of Patince Kupele has two thermal lakes that attract visitors.

Patince

▣ **Thermal lakes,** two small lakes good for swimming and boating.

Follow the curve to the right before the road reaches Žitava ∼ then straight to **Radvan** nad Dunajom.

Radvan

Tip: Radvan has several restaurants where one can get good meals.

Continue along the moderately-busy No. 63 to Moca.

Moča

Moča to Esztergom   **30.5 km**

300 meters after entering Moča, turn right and leave the main road ∼ follow the small street ∼ stay right ∼ until you reach the dam

∼ to the left of the dam along the river there is a lightly-traveled country lane ∼ which you can follow straight downriver ∼ until you reach **Kravany nad Dunajor**.

Kravany nad Dunajor

Stay on the same road next to the dike ∼ at a 40 km/h speed limit sign at the edge of the village turn onto the paved dike track ∼ and continue straight along the dike ∼ just before Čenkov turn right where the dike road meets the No. 63 main road ∼ turn right on the road ∼ and follow it straight to Muzla.

Čenkov

Tip: From here you can choose between the main route on the dike along the river and then riding through the village of Obid, or staying on the No. 63 main road as far as Mužla.

Alternate route through Mužla

If you choose the alternative route, stay on the moderately-busy No. 63 road ∼ into the town of **Mužla** (which also has overnight accommodations) ∼ at the intersection turn right towards **Štúrovo**. After about 3.7 kilometers you come to the place where the main route intersects with the No. 63.

To stay on the main route, in Čenkov turn right after you see a rest-area on the left side ∼ and straight. At first the road is unpaved ∼ after 2.3 kilometers switch to the unpaved dike -road and continue straight ahead ∼ straight, until you see a factory building on the left side at the foot of the dam ∼ turn left there, away from the dam ∼ and straight onto a paved farm lane ∼ stay right and then make a 45° left turn and then straight into the village of **Obid**.

Obid

At the church turn right and follow the course of the road through the village ∼ until you run into the main road again

Follow the main road straight east ∼ after several kilometers you will reach the city of Štúrovo.

Štúrovo

This city is named after the Slovak writer, linguist and nationalist L'udovít Štúr, who is credited with creating the modern Slovak language. He was also a politician and revolutionary, and died at the age of 40 in 1856 in Modra, north of Bratislava.

Tip: Before you leave Štúrovo, take the time to explore the city and enjoy the fine views of the basilica at Esztergom, across the river.

Follow the main road proceed to the Danube river bridge and the border controls ∼ after crossing the border proceed across the bridge into Hungary ∼ after the

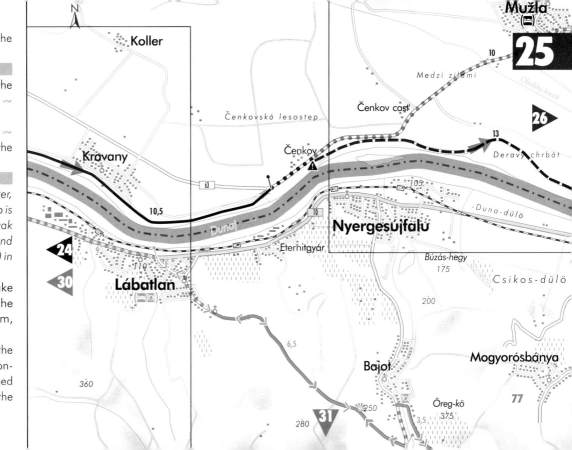

bridge take the ramp to the left downwards ～ take the small bridge across the canal in front of the Hotel Esztergom and ride along the river bank to the Esztergom ship landings ～ and turn left.

Esztergom   **citymap see page 92**
Postal code: 2500; Phone area code: 33

🛈 **Gran Tours**, Széchenyi tér 25. ☏ 417052

🏛 **Christian Museum** (Keresztény-Múzeum), Mindszenty tér 2, Open: 10-17. The museum in the former bishops palace holds paintings, sculptures, gobelins, tapestries and porcelain made by important Hungarian, German, Austrian and Italian masters.

🏛 **Cathedral treasure**, Szent István tér, Open: Tues-Sun 9-16: 30, ☏ 402-353

🏛 **Local history museum Balassa-Bálint**, Mindszenty tér, Open: Tues-Sun 10-17, ☏ 413-185. Overview of the city's 1,000-year history.

🏛 **Danube museum**, Kölcsey F. út 2, Open: Nov-April, Mon-Sun 10-16, May-Oct, 10-18, ☏ 500-250

🏛 **Castle museum**, Szent István tér 1, Open: Tues-Sun 10-18, ☏ 315-986. Exhibits about the history of Esztergom Castle.

🛖 **Royal palace**, Szent István tér. A collection of stone monuments remains from the original palace built by King Belas III

(1172-96). The palace chapel with its rose window is one of the most beautiful Romanesque structures in Hungary. The upper floor contains renaissance chambers from János Vitéz, humanist and archbishop.

🛖 **Basilica**, Szent István tér, Open: Mon-Sun 6-16:30, ☏ 411-895. The original Adalbert cathedral built by King Stephan was heavily damaged during the Turkish wars. In 1822 construction began on what was to be the largest church in Hungary, commensurate with the importance of the Gran bishopric. The main alter of Carrara marble was designed by Pietro Bonani. The church was consecrated in 1856 at a ceremony for which Franz Liszt wrote his "Gran Mass."

🛖 **Water city** (Víziváros), at the foot of the fortress and along the Little Danube. Among the most noteworthy buildings in the old city center are the 18th century parish church (Pázmány Péter út) in the water city, the central church (Pór Antal tér), which is one of the prettiest baroque structures in the city (1757-62), and the Greek-orthodox church (Kossuth Lajos u. 60).

✱ **Danube passenger ships to** Budapest, Mahart Co., Budapest, ☏ 1/318-1223, bicycles may be transported if space allows. Groups should make reservations (Mahart: 413531)

▱ City beaches and thermal baths, Bajcsy-Zsilinszky út 14, ☏ 403-957

Tip: To connect with the main route to Budapest simply proceed straight after crossing the bridge, on the Táncsics Mihály u. Then cross the Bottyán hid bridge and then turn left on the path along the Danube Kis-Duna Sétány.

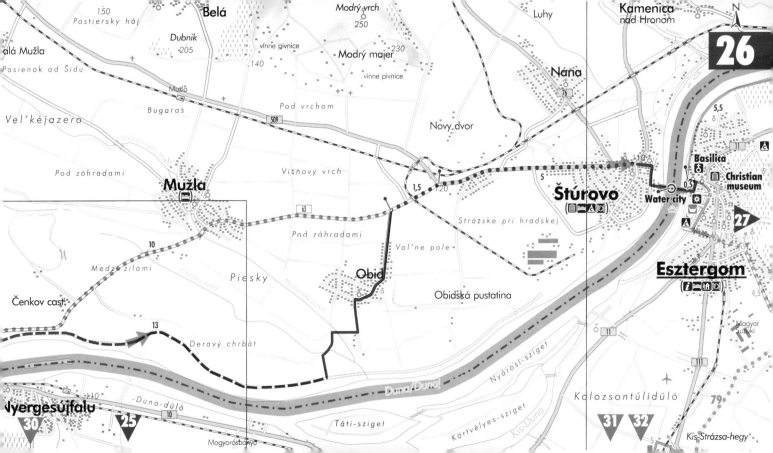

Komárom to Esztergom (H)

74 km

The route immediately after Komárom leads into an idyllic and quiet countryside away from the Danube. This stage of the ride offers a wealth of delightful landscapes and interesting cultural sites. These detours also provide more interesting scenery and cultural sites: the venerable old city of Tata at the feet of the Gerecse mountains and the "Alten See" beneath the vineyards over the Danube river valley. The route has a few moderate climbs which are rewarded by excellent views into the surrounding landscape and the exciting ride back into the valley. The last kilometers pass through Lábatlan and Tokod before arriving in the "Hungarian Rome," as the city of Esztergom is sometimes called.

This part of the route has sections with numerous hills and climbs, and mostly follows lightly-traveled country roads. The main exception is around Süttö, where the bicycle route runs along the B 10 main road.

Komárom

Ppstal code: 2900; Phone area code: 34

🛈 **Tourinform**, Igmándi út 2, ✆ 540-590, www.komarom.hu

🏛 **Klapka György Museum**, Kelemen Lásló u. 22, ✆ 344697, Open: 26 April-Sept Tues-Sun 10-18, Oct-25 April Tues-Sun 10-16. Frescoes and other artifacts found at Brigetio, sarcophagi with human remains, gold jewelry and items made of glass and bronze.

🏛 **Maritime Museum**, Szabadság tér 1 (town hall), ✆ 541340, Open: 26 April-Sept Tues-Sun 10-18, Oct-25 April Tues-Sun 10-16

⛏ **Fortress Igmánd** (Roman lapidarium), Igmándi eröd, ✆ 5085097, Open: 26 April-Sept 10-16, closed in the winter. Exhibits of ancient stone work, inscribed grave stones, plus sarcophagi and altar blocks.

⛏ **Fort Monostor**, Monostori Eröd, Dunapart, ✆ 540-582 Open: 15 March-Okt, Mon-Sun 9-17. The Monostor fortress is the largest modern fortification in central Europe. Built between 1850 and 1871, it consists of a complex network of fortification walls, moats and underground bunkers. Today it is maintained as a memorial to Hungary's military history.

⛏ **Roman Catholic Church**, Szent László utca. Significant example of modern Hungarian church architecture City hall, Hösök tere. Neo-baroque town hall.

📷 **Thermal baths and campground**, Táncsics M. út 34-36, ✆ 342551. Various facilities, including six pools with water of various temperatures.

Komárom to Tata   18.5 km

Tip: Before you set off from Komárom for this stage, be sure to buy sufficient food and beverages. The route to Tata is strenuous and there are no stores or restaurants along the way.

Ride out of Komárom on the B°10 national road ~ there is a bicycle path to the left of the road as far as the railroad ~ then on the bicycle lane to the turnoff to the right, to Mocsa ~ ride through the village of **Szöny** ~ after the bridge turn left towards Tata ~ soon the road starts to pass vineyards ~ and becomes hillier for the rest of the almost 20-kilometer distance to Tata.

Kakas útca meets **Komáromi útca** ~ go straight at the large intersection ~ turn left on **Rakoczi utca** before the church ~ and follow the course of the road ~ turn left at the next intersection ~ then take the first right ~ and follow this street in a long curve to the right around the old castle ~ this is the **Bartók B. u.** ~ and then turn right on Alkotmary u. ~ and proceed straight to **Ady Endre utca**.

Tata

Postal code: 2890; Phone area code: 34

🛈 **Tourinform**, Ady Endre u. 9, ✆ 586-046

🏛 **Hungarian-German Museum**, Alkotmány u. 1, ✆ 487682, Open: 15 April-31 Oct, Tues-Sun 10-18. History and folklore about Hungaro-Germans, on display in the Miklós Mill (1760).

🏛 **Kuny Domonkos Museum**, Öregvár (old castle), ✆ 487-888, Open: May-Oct, 10-18. Archaeological artifacts, faience, ceramic from Tata and works by the painter Ferenc Martyn.

🏛 **Museum for Greek/Roman castings**, Hösök tere, ✆ 487888 or 381251, Open: Tues-Sun 10-18. A valuable collection of antique sculptures, housed in the former synagogue.

⛏ **Old castle** (Öregvár), on the lakefront. The original 13th century Gothic structure was expanded in the renaissance style by King Matthias Corvinus (1440-90). Further renovations and additions in the 19th century.

⛏ **Eszterházy palace**, Hösök tere, Seeuferpromenade, ✆ 380-124. Furnished in the 17th century plain style by Jakob Fellner, who worked for the prince's family and helped shape the city's appearance. Today the building serves as a hospital.

- 🟦 **Holy Cross parish church** (Szentkereszt templom), Kossuth tér. Late-baroque church built 1751-85 by Anton Pilgram, Jakob Fellner and Josef Großmann.
- ❇️ **Clock tower**, Országgyülés tér (parliament square). Octagonal wooden tower (1763), formerly the city prison, was built by the master carpenter Josef Eder.
- ❇️ **Watermills**, old lake front (Öregtó). The baroque Cifra Mill (1753) stands on the eastern shore of the lake, not far from the Miklós Mill built in 1760 by Fellner.
- ❇️ **Calvary Hill**, Fekete út, olive orchards and viewing tower, ✆ 384306.
- 🔺 **English Garden** (Néppark), east of the old lake. Nature preserve and recreation area in an old English garden.
- ▭ **Fenyes spa and camping**, ✆ 588-144
- ▭ **Public swimming pool**, Cseke-tó
- ▭ **Kristály pool**, Erzsébet tér, ✆ 381362 or 587377
- 🚲 **Bike rental**, ✆ 0620-4320420
- 🚲 **Bike shop**, Vértesszölösi u. 47, ✆ 487490

The old city of Tata lies at the feet of the Gerecse and Vértes mountains. Due to its many lakes, natural springs and canals this city on the water enjoys a relaxing atmosphere. Tata

Old Lake in Tata

is centered around the Old Lake (Öreg-tó) and Tata Castle. The region was settled in the Stone Age, as evidenced by archaeological finds at Vértesszölös 5 kilometers distant.

Hungarians started moving to areas around the lakes in the 10th century. The earliest known official record of the area mentions the existence a small settlement and a Benedictine abbey in the 11th century. By the 14th century there were two villages named Tata and separated by a low-lying swamp. Since 1397 Tata has been, along with Buda and Visegrád, a favorite residence of the kings.

In the 14th century Hungary's only water-castle was built on the shores of the Öreg-tó. In 1526 the town fell to the Turks during their first invasion, was retaken by the Emperor and then repeatedly recaptured by the Turkish armies. The heavy fighting caused severe damage to the castle as well as the city and its many mills. Towards the end of the 17th century the castle was called the "puszta vár", which means "desolate castle."

After 1727 the town became the property of the Esterházy family. It wished to raze the castle and replace it with a baroque palace, but was unable to finance the project. Instead, the family expanded the castle with a new addition. The Habsburg Kaiser Francis I signed the Peace of Schönbrunn while staying here in the fall of 1809.

The castle and the entire grounds remained the property of the Esterházy family until 1945. In 1965 it became the property of the Hungarian Museum. Because the castle moat often served as its garbage dump, excavations on the site have turned up large amounts of weapons, broken armor, cannons and cannonballs as well as boots, shoes and other refuse.

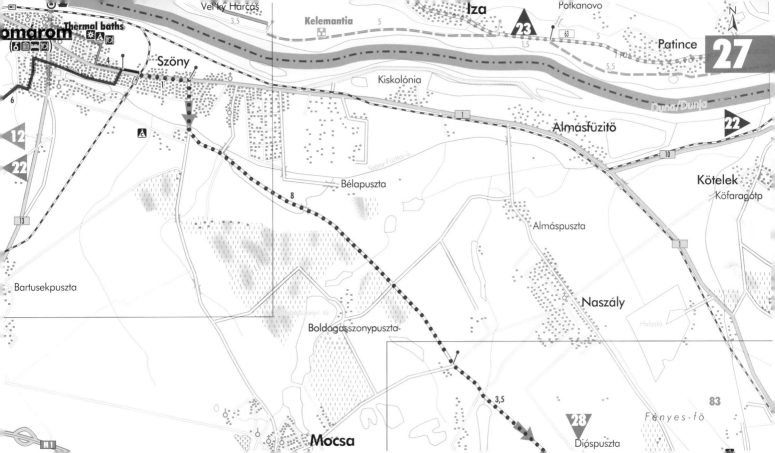

Vel'ký Harčáš

Iza

Potkanovo

Kelemantia

23

63

Patince

27

5

Kiskolónia

Szöny

Duna/Dunja

omarom

Thermal baths

4

1

1

Almásfüzitö

22

12

6

Bélapuszta

10

Kötelek

Köfaragótp

22

13

Szöny-Fuzitor-á

8

Almáspuszta

Naszály

Bartusekpuszta

Boldogasszonyi-fö

Halastó

Boldogasszonypuszta

3,5

Mocsa

28

Dióspuszta

83

Fényes-fö

M1

Between the castle and the lake there is a magnificent promenade through the grounds. It is open to bicyclists.

To enter the Kuny Domokos Museum, one walks up the red marble steps to the terrace, where there is a café and the museum entrance

Another interesting museum is the "Hungaro-German Museum" in the Miklós Mill. The mill is designated a historic landmark and recalls the important role that mills played in Tata's development. During and after the Turkish wars, the population of Tata declined severely. Under the Esterházy family many Germans settled in the area.

On the smaller lake, the Cseke-tó, there is a public park configured as an English garden with small waterfalls and an intricate network of small paths. The mock ruins of a three-nave church were reconstructed in the park using old Roman grave stones and Romanesque

Old castle on the lakefront

blocks from the Vértesszentkereszt Benedictine abbey.

Of the man old water mills, the oldest is believed to be the baroque "Cifra Mill." The octagonal clock-tower on the Landtagsplatz was built without a single piece of iron hardware by the master carpenter Josef Eder in 1763.

Tip: Before getting started from Tata, one should not neglect the opportunity to visit Vértesszölös, the site where traces have been found of Stone Age community. The site can be reached by riding out of town on Ady Endre út, where the main Komtourist office is located. The Vértesszölös site is about 7 kilometers away.

In the footsteps of our ancestry   14 km

Ride out Vértesszölössi út, which is the extension of Ady Endre út. It runs along the side of the lake, until you reach the village of Vértesszölös. The 750-meter hike to the location of the oldest hominid footprint found in Europe starts about half a kilometer past the Vértesszölös-sign.

Vértesszölös

✠ Excavations, Múzeum u. 1., ✆ 710-350, Site where stone age tools, fire-sites and a skull fragment were found. One of the oldest sites testifying to early man's use of fire. Open: 1 April-15 Oct, Tues-Fri 10-15, Sat-Sun 10-18.

An archaeological team working under the guidance of Ladislav Vertés between 1962 and 1968 found footprints and signs of habitation by late Neanderthal and early Homo Sapiens. Estimated to be about 500,000 years old, it is the oldest such site ever found in central Europe.

The early humans who lived then were hunter-gatherers who lived in caves. The epoch is known as the "pebble culture," which refers to the simple flint-stones which these cave dwellers used as early humans started learning how to improve and file their tools. Numerous sites in this area testify that our ancestors settled here at a very early period, drawn perhaps by the hot springs that may have made their lives somewhat more comfortable.

Old Castle in Tata

Water and wind shaped the terrain over the eons. Half-a-million years ago the hollows started to fill with loam, resulting in the current landscape. Paleologists had to dig through four layers of civilization to reach the pre-historic sites they hoped to find.

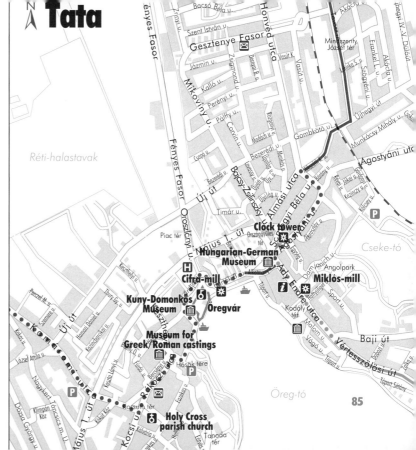

Several interesting finds were uncovered at Vértesszölös. Today some of them can be seen in their original locations, which are protected by buildings with large windows that keep the elements away from the sites. The first building contains the cave with its fireplace, the remains of animal bones and assorted stone tools. Noteworthy is that the flintstones, large numbers of which have been found here, do not fit this region geographically. The occupants evidently recognized the utility of different kinds of stones, collected them elsewhere and brought them here. A second site shows the petrified 300,000 year-old footprints of early humans and animals. These enable scientists to draw conclusions about the size and shape of the people who lived here. Plaster casts of the footprints can be seen in one of the exhibit cases

After Tata return the same way you arrived. If you have time, consider taking a swim in the warm lakes before continuing the ride.

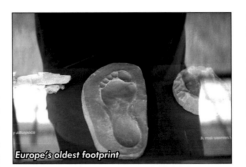
Europe's oldest footprint

Tata to Lábatlan   22.5 km

Turn left on **Ady Endre utca** ~ on the right side is **Országgyülés tér** ~ at the eight-sided wooden tower go straight on **Agostyáni u.** ~ turn left ~ then right on **Mikszáth K. utca** ~ after the railroad crossing take the first street to the left, **Tavasz utca** ~ then straight ahead to the main road and then right towards **Szomód** ~ and immediately stay to the right again.

Szomód

Tip: The route passes through some exceptionally scenic countryside on the way to Szomód and Dunaszentmiklós, but it is also quite strenuous. This is where a little training before the trip pays off.

Szomód is the name of the first village after Tata ~ turn right at the first church ~ and proceed over the hills toward **Dunaszent-miklós**.

Dunaszentmiklós

The village Dunaszentmiklós has a significant German-speaking population, and has a number of homes that offer rooms to rent.

Tip: The views in Dunaszentmiklós are breathtaking, extending far across the river and into Slovakia to the north

Ride along the village main street ~ pass to the right of the church ~ and through a 45° left turn ~ the road becomes narrower as it leaves Dunaszentmiklós.

A Tip: The serpentine descent into the Danube river valley is steep and fast and demands full attention. The road is paved, but the asphalt is in poor condition. Keep a sharp eye open for potholes and cracks!

The route passes a large winery ~ turn right at the bottom of the descent, onto the B10

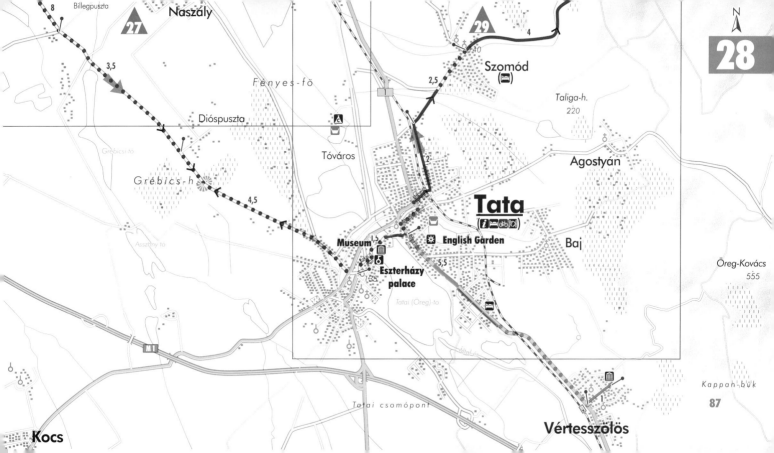

Billegpuszta
8

Naszály

27

3,5

Fényes-fő

Dióspuszta

Tóváros

Grébicsi-tó

Grébics-h

4,5

Asszony-tó

Museum

Eszterházy
palace

29

4

Szomód

2,5

Taliga-h.
220

2

Agostyán

Tata

ⓘ 🛏 ♿ 📷

English Garden

Baj

Öreg-Kovács
555

5,5

Tatai (Öreg)-tó

M1

Tatai csomópont

Kocs

Vértesszőlős

Kappan-bükk

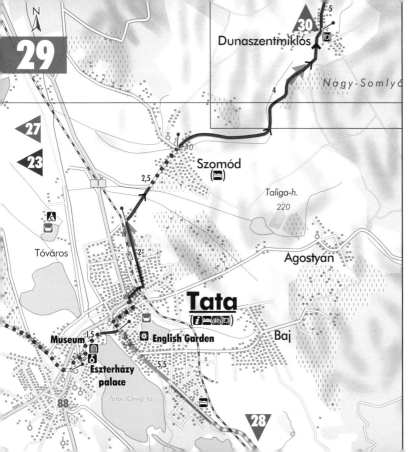

national road ∿ and proceed with the traffic for several kilometers to the village of **Süttö** and on to **Lábatlan**.

Lábatlan

Lábatlan to Tokod   7.5 km

200 meters past the church in Lábatlan turn right at the sign marking the way to Bajót.

At the edge of Lábatlan pass under the rusty aerial tramway used to transport chalk from a nearby quarry down to the river. The quarry dominates the landscape here.

After the entrance to the quarry, ride through a woods ∿ the road is hilly ∿ as it leads up to a wide pass that connects two wooded ridges ∿ the route leads to the ridge on the left, which is named **Öreg-kö** ∿ after the scenic lookout the road goes downhill through many sharp curves. Be prepared to use your brakes frequently ∿ at the intersection turn left towards **Nyergesújfalu** and **Bajót**.

Bajót

Proceed straight into the center of Bajot ∿ and soon come to a junction ∿ where a traffic sign points towards Tokod ∿ at this junction make the sharp turn to the right∿ and then follow the course of the road ∿ as it heads first up hill and then downhill ∿ past a monastery ∿ until you reach another junction ∿ where you turn left towards Tát ∿ the road goes through a left turn ∿ and you come to another junction ∿ turn right there ∿ and soon you will ride into the village of Tokod.

Tokod

Tokod to Esztergom   15.5 km

At the intersection turn right towards Tokod and ride into the

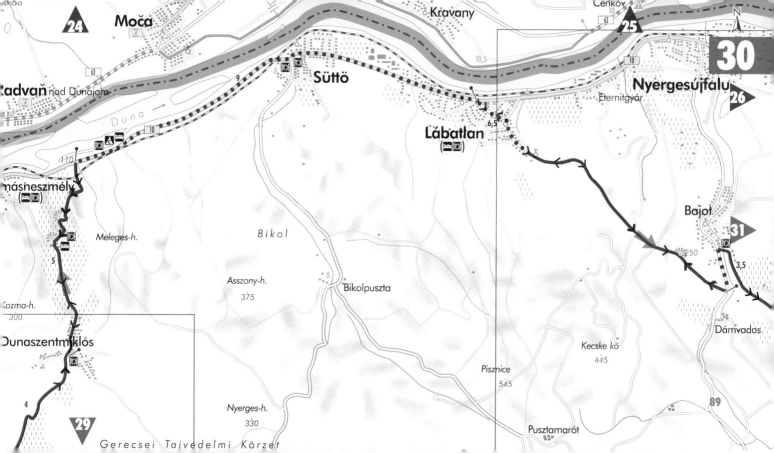

town ～ turn left at the church and then straight ahead through an industrial area to the No. 10 national road ～ turn right and proceed 150 meters before making a left turn on a small village street ～ at first this street is paved before it turns to gravel ～ proceed straight ～ turn right at the railroad and take the unpaved path that runs parallel to the rail-line ～ after about 1.5 kilometers go straight across the railroad ～ at the intersection continue straight on an unpaved village street～ which soon has a paved surface. Proceed straight onto the next gravel stretch which again returns to the railroad ～ cross the railroad again and go straight on the paved street ～ turn right at the

intersection with the "Yield" sign ～ cross the railroad yet again and proceed straight ahead ～ you come to a large traffic circle ～ which you go straight through ～ and after about 500 meters turn left ～ a large traffic sign points towards Esztergom ～ at the next T-intersection turn left towards Esztergom ～ at the next small intersection keep going straight ～ and on to another traffic circle ～ for a short distance straight ahead ～ towards the center ～at the next small intersection keep going straight ～ and on to another traffic circle ～ for a short distance straight ahead ～ then left on **Àrok utca** ～ you come to a bridge ～ turn right ～ and ride along the **Kis Duna** towards the center of **Esztergom** ～ cross **Lorinc u.** ～ the center of town is now to the right ～ proceed straight to **Kossuth hid**.

Esztergom

Postal code: 2500; Phone area code: 33

🆔 **Gran Tours**, Széchenyi tér 25. ☎ 417052

🏛 **Christian Museum** (Keresztény-Múzeum), Mindszenty tér 2, Open: 10-17. The museum in the former bishops palace holds paintings, sculptures, gobelins, tapestries and porcelain made

Basilica in Esztergom

by important Hungarian, German, Austrian and Italian masters.

🏛 **Cathedral treasure**, Szent István tér, Open: Tues-Sun 9-16: 30, ☎ 402-353

🏛 **Local history museum Balassa-Bálint**, Mindszenty tér, Open: Tues-Sun 10-17, ☎ 413-185. Overview of the city's 1,000-year history.

🏛 **Danube museum**, Kölcsey F. út 2, Open: Nov-April, Mon-Sun 10-16, May-Oct, 10-18, ☎ 500-250

🏛 **Castle museum**, Szent István tér 1, Open: Tues-Sun 10-18, ☎ 315-986. Exhibits about the history of Esztergom Castle.

⬛ **Royal palace**, Szent István tér. A collection of stone monuments remains from the original palace built by King Belas III (1172-96). The palace chapel with its rose window is one of the most beautiful Romanesque structures in Hungary. The

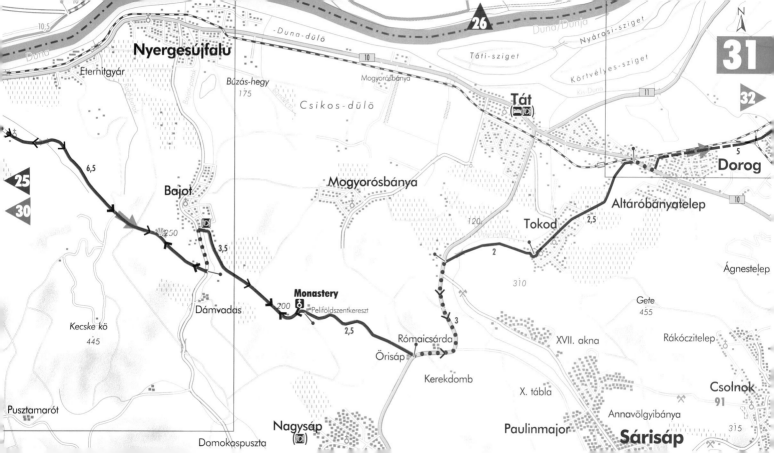

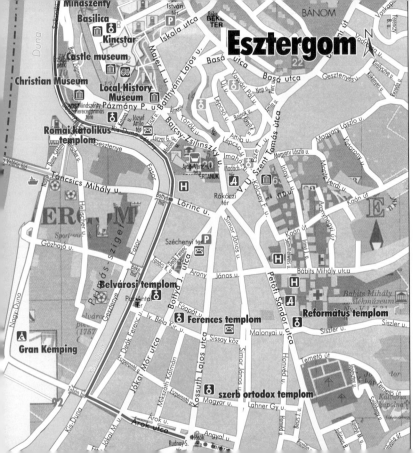

Esztergom

Minaszenty
Basilica
Kincstar
Castle museum
Christian Museum
Local History Museum
Római katolikus templom
Belvárosi templom
Ferences templom
Gran Kemping
Református templom
szerb ortodox templom

Basilica in Esztergom

upper floor contains renaissance chambers from János Vitéz, humanist and archbishop.

Basilica, Szent István tér, Open: Mon-Sun 6-16:30, ☎ 411-895. The original Adalbert cathedral built by King Stephan was heavily damaged during the Turkish wars. In 1822 construction began on what was to be the largest church in Hungary, commensurate with the importance of the Gran bishopric. The main alter of Carrara marble was designed by Pietro Bonani. The church was consecrated in 1856 in a ceremony for which Franz Liszt wrote his "Gran Mass."

Water city (Víziváros), at the foot of the fortress and along the Little Danube. Among the most noteworthy buildings in the old city center are the 18th century parish church (Pázmány Péter út) in the water city, the central church (Pór Antal tér), which is one of the prettiest baroque structures in the city (1757-62), and the Greek-orthodox church (Kossuth Lajos u. 60).

- ❌ **Danube passenger ships to** Budapest, Fa. Mahart, Budapest, ✆ 1/318-1223, bicycles may be transported if space allows. Groups should make reservations (Mahart: 413531)
- ✉ City beaches and thermal baths, Bajcsy-Zsilinszky út 14, ✆ 403-957

The Hungarian writer Mihály Babits called Esztergom "Hungary's Rome." Others, like the country's communists, saw Esztergom as the "city of the black reaction." Both views arise from the city's role as the Roman Catholic church's capital in Hungary. The church's highest primate, the Archbishop of Esztergom, has been based here since the 11th century.

Excavations have shown that the castle mountain and surroundings were first settled in the Stone Age. The Romans fortified the mountain to protect their border.

Esztergom is one of the oldest cities in Hungary. It is even mentioned, as the "Etzelsburg", in the Song of the Nibelungen.

After the Magyars moved into the region in the 10th century, Esztergom became the center of the Hungarian nation. In the year 1000, Hungary's first king, Stephan the Holy, was crowned here. The city enjoyed its heyday during the reign of King Béla IV. He hired famous foreign architects and artists to design and build his palace and the castle chapel, another of the city's Roman Catholic landmarks. In 1249, after the Mongol invasion, King Béla VI moved his residence from Esztergom to Buda.

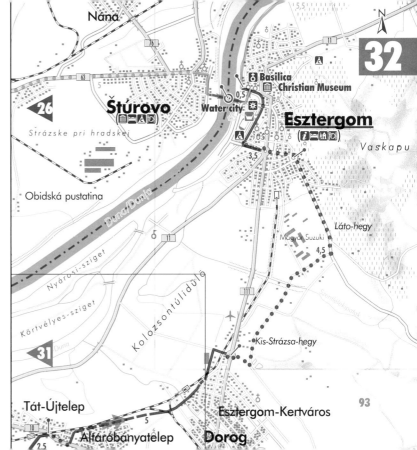

The archbishop of Esztergom and other Hungarian clerics then moved into the abandoned royal palace. The city enjoyed a second heyday during the time of János Vitéz, an archbishop during the renaissance. In the 13th century, the city was occupied by the Tartars, and in the 16th century it was the Turks, who remained in Esztergom until 1683. When they were finally driven out, Esztergom was in ruins, with a population of just 400. The city began to recover only after the basilica had been built and the archbishops returned.

The current city actually consists of three settlements that were united as a single entity in 1895 under the name Esztergom.

It was also in 1895 that the Maria Valeria Bridge across the Danube was built. It was de-stroyed in World War II, and not rebuilt until 2001. Today it serves as the border crossing to the Slovak town of Stúrovo.

The most impressive building in the city is the huge basilica dedicated to St. Adalbert. It is the largest church in Hungary and dominates the views from the surrounding countryside. It was under construction from 1822 to 1869, but was consecrated 13 years before its completion. Franz Liszt composed his well-known Gran Mass for the occasion.

The church was heavily damaged during WWII. The altar-piece in the choir nave is believed to the largest of its kind in the world. Painted by the Italian Grigoletti, it measures 13 x 6.5 meters and is based on the Titian painting, "Ascension of Mary", which hangs in the Frari church in Venice.

The dome of the church is open to the public in the summer, and offers outstanding views. The basilica also houses Hungary's largest collection of church art, while the diocese library is among the best in the country. The library is not open to the public.

Esztergom to Budapest

on the right bank: 70 km
on the left bank: 77 km

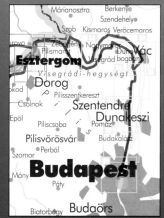

The cultural highlights along this last stage to Budapest are the cities of Visegrád and Szentendre. The royal palace and the castle in Visegrád dominate the impressive bend in the river, the "knee" of the Danube. The open-air museum and the baroque city center of Szentendre tempt the traveler to pause once more before pushing on to the final goal of this tour, the Hungarian capital and Danube metropolis of Budapest. This stage could hardly be more varied. At times the route puts the bicyclist in traffic on the busy B10, at other times it follows very-lightly traveled country lanes like, for instance on the Szentendrei Sziget, or simple farm tracks and well-made bicycle paths into Budapest. There are two possible routes through the Danube's knee. One goes from Visegrád via Szigetmonostor and Szentendre into the center of Budapest; the other takes the left bank of the Danube from Szob through Nagymaros to Vác before it crosses onto the Szentendrei Sziget. More comfortable, but just as scenic, is to take a ship down the river.

Esztergom to Pilismarót on the right bank — 12.5 km

Return to the riverside beneath the cathedral ~ there is a nice paved bicycle path for several kilometers down the Danube's shore ~ go straight until you come to the B 11 national road ~ and continue with traffic on the B 11.

Tip: **Before one reaches** Pilismarót, there is a road to the left that leads down to the ferry to Szob. Here one must decide whether to continue on the right bank of the river or cross to the left bank. The right side has more motorized traffic. The Danube bicycle route runs along both sides – on the right side it is posted between Szentendre and Budapest, while on the left side it is posted after Zebegény.

Szob to Vác on the left bank — 31.5 km

Turn left off the No. 11 national road and ride down to the ferry. The road is marked by a sign "Rév."

Szob

🚢 **Pilismarót-Szob ferry,** Open: 27/370042, 30/9144195, 6: 10-19:50, departs hourly.

🚉 **Szob train station** (only with valid ticket)

At the ferry landing in Szob immediately turn right on the paved bicycle path along the Danube ~ at the church turn left on the cobblestone street ~ after 100 meters turn right on a paved street ~ after 300 meters go underneath the railroad ~ and then turn right ~ at the next intersection turn right again on the No. 12 national road, towards Vác ~ the next town is Zebegény with its villas ~ after the underpass for the railroad there is a bicycle path on the right side, and the first Danube bicycle route signs ~ after about 2 kilometers on the bicycle path there is a short piece on the main road ~ after about 1 kilometer the bicycle path resumes on the right side of the road and continues along the river ~ you are now in the town limits of **Nagymaros.**

Nagymaros

🚢 **Ferry Nagymaros-Visegrád,** Rév út (ferry landing), ☎ 26/ 398344, Open: 6:35 – 19:35, departures every 20-40 minutes.

Tip: Here you have the option of taking the ferry to Visegrád and switching to the other side of the Danube.

The bicycle route leads out of the town and along the Danube ~ and past a campground ~ ride towards Nagymaros on a path made of concrete slabs through fields between the Danube and the main road ~ you come to a bridge ~ ride up onto the bridge and then take the dam track ~ as it curves to the left around the village of **Kismaros** ~ ride up to the national road and turn right ~ a short distance with traffic ~ between Kismaros and Veröcemaros there is a short bicycle path on the right side ~ and ride with traffic through **Veröce.**

Veröcemaros

The bicycle path resumes on the left side of the road at the edge of Veröcemaros ~ before it reaches Vác the route runs between the main road and the railroad ~ it passes underneath the road ~ stay to the right of the railroad and turn right just before the main road ~ and follow the path ~ stay right ~ at the next small fork go left ~ until you come to another small

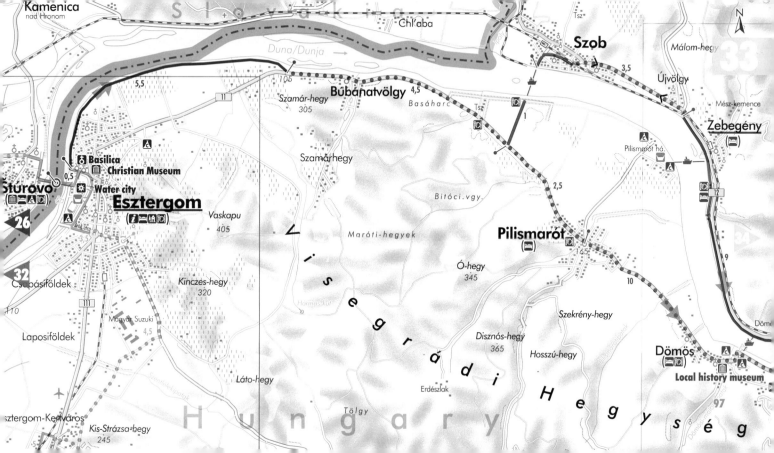

street ～ turn left here and then immediately right ～ onto a marked bicycle/pedestrian path ～ to the left pass the victory arch which is on a parallel street ～ proceed on the bicycle path on the banks of the Danube ～ to reach the ferry landing.

Vác

Postal code: 2600; Phone area code: 27

🛈 **Tourinform**, Március 15 Tér 16-18, ☎ 316-160

⛴ **Ferry to Szentendrei Sziget**, ☎ 26/386560, May-Sept, 6-21, April, Oct, 6-20, Nov-March, 6-19, continuous operation with departures every 20-40 minutes.

⛴ **Danube shipping**, Mahart (Co.), ☎ 1/1381223, Open: 24 May-24 Aug, departures to Budapest Mon-Sun 18:10. Bicycles will be transported if space is available. Groups must make reservations.

🏛 **Tragor Ignác Museum**, Zrínyi út 41/A, ☎ 500750, March-Sept, Tues-Sun, 10-18. Archaeological artifacts, folk art and items from the revolution of 1848.

🔳 **Cathedral**, Március 15.-e tér. The pride of the city was built 1763-77 by Isidore Canevale. Frescoes in the choir and dome by Franz Anton Maulbertsch. The crypt has valuable renaissance and baroque wrought iron works.

🔳 **Franciscan church**, Géza király tér 12. Construction of this in-

Basilca, Vác

teresting baroque church began in 1721 and took about 30 years to complete.

🔳 **Botanic garden Vácrátót** (Arborétum), 13 south-west

✳ **Victory arch** (Diadalív), Köztársaság út 69. City residents refer to the monument simply as the "stone arch." Built in 1764 for a visit by Empress Maria Theresa, it is the only arch of its kind in Hungary.

✳ **Main square** (Március 15.-e tér). A handsome square with numerous historic baroque buildings.

💬 **Public pool**, Ady Endre sétány 16

💬 **Beach**, Szentháromság tér 1

King Stephan I established a bishopric here in the 11th century and Vác was officially documented for the first time in 1075. Long a residence for the local nobility, the town today is known for its baroque architecture and works of art. For example, Vác's central square in Hungary's only baroque city square. Another equally noteworthy structure is the victory arch at the edge of the upper city (Felsövarós), built to honor a visit by Maria Theresa. The 18th century post-baroque cathedral was designed by the Viennese court architect Isidore Caneval, who was inspired by a neo classical style developed in France.

Vác is a city where old and new stand side-by-side. On the one hand, the old baroque monuments and structures lend the town an air of stately idleness, while on the other hand Vác is also a lively university town, and a cultural and economic center with a thriving and growing tourism industry.

Take the ferry to the **Szentendrei Sziget** ～ and then continue on a rural road to **Tahitót-falu** ～ ride straight into the town, to a square with a monument, where the left-bank route converges with the right-bank route coming from **Visegrad**.

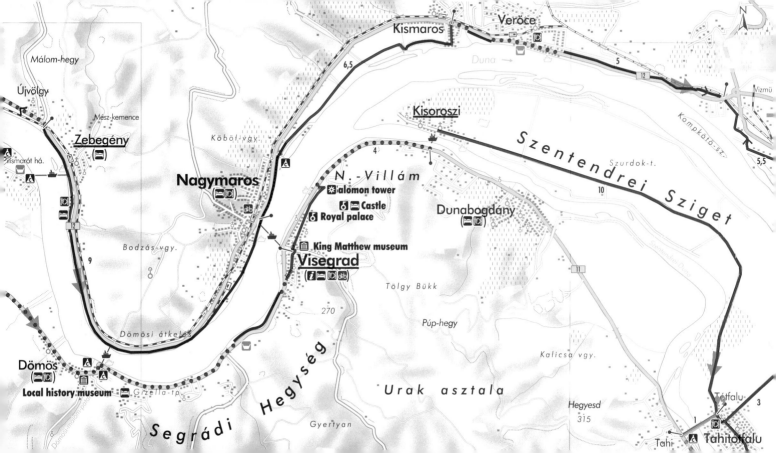

Málom-hegy

Újvölgy

Zebegény

Mész-kemence

Nismaróti há.

Kőböl-vgy.

Nagymaros

Bodzás-vgy.

9

Dömösi átkelés

Dömös

Local history museum

Gizella-tp.

S e g r á d i   H e g y s é g

Gyertyan

Kismaros

Veröce

Duna →

6,5

5

12

Kisoroszi

4

N.-Villám

☀ alomon tower

🔰 Castle

Royal palace

🏛 King Matthew museum

Visegrad

Dunabogdány

S z e n t e n d r e i   S z i g e t

Szurdok-t.

Kompkötő-sz.

5,5

10

270

Tölgy Bükk

Púp-hegy

U r a k   a s z t a l a

Kalicsa vgy.

Hegyesd
315

11

Vízmű

Tótfalu

3

1

Tahi

Tahitotfalu

N

The right bank
from Pilismarót to Visegrad   10 km

Tip: Maps 33 and 34 show this part of the right bank route.

Tip: In Pilismarót, turn left at the church, towards the Danube. The beach and a campground are about 2 kilometers from the town.

Continue along the No. 11 main road for a short stretch to reach Dömös.

Dömös

Postal code: 2027; Phone area code: 033

🏛 Local history museum, in the cultural center, Táncsics M. út 2, ☎ 507050, Open: Tues-Sat 8-16, Sun 10-15. Local history exhibitions and creative arts.

Starting in Dömös the bicycle route runs directly adjacent to the Danube on the No. 11 main road through the Danube's famous "knee." This unique scenery is best seen from a ship on the river.

The Danube Bend

The knee of the Danube is, along with Lake Balaton, one of the most scenic areas of Hun-

View in Vác

gary. Over a distance of about 20 kilometers, the river breaks through steep mountain sides and cliffs, some of which are formed of volcanic rock and soft chalk. The dark slopes and the strangely-formed rocks provide a romantic landscape.

The river curves through a wide bend as it passes through the mountains and then turns southward and divides into two streams as it passes around Szentendre Island (Saint Andrä Island). The main arm of the Danube – which is also called the Vacer – is used by international shipping while the smaller arm carries just a third as much water.

The right bank is dominated by the Visegrád Mountains and the Pilis Mountains rising into the blue Magyar skies. On the left bank stretch the foothills of the Börzsöny Mountains. Numerous hiking paths criss-cross the region, dotted with rest-areas and picnic-sites. The entire Hungarian highlands make a completely different impression than the wide expanses of the Puszta plains further east. And because this part of the Danube's passage through Hungary played such an important role in the country's history, the area is also rich with historic monuments and sites that reflect its culture and heritage.

In the last century before Christ, Illyrian-Celtic tribes began settling in the area, the Latin name for the city Szentendre was Ulcisia Castra, derived from the Celtic "Ulk".

The Romans were the first to leave lasting marks on the region. Their influence changed the lives of indigenous people and gave the Danube a new importance. During the Roman times, the river formed the Empire's border and defense against barbarian invaders.

Three-and-a-half kilometers after Dömös the route passes the Visegrád public pool ∿ where the bicycle route resumes at a lower level to the left of the main roadway ∿ and offers fine views of the castle at Visegrád ∿ followed by a short stretch on the main road ∿ just before the playing field turn to the right onto **Fö út** ∿ which leads straight into Visegrád and past the royal palace.

Visegrád
Postal code: 2025; Phone area code: 26

🛈 Visegrád Tours, Rév u. 15 (across from the ferry), ☎ 398160

⛴ Visegrád-Nagymaros ferry, Rév út (ferry landing), ☎ 26/ 398344, hourly. continuous departures between 6:35 and 19:35.

🏛 King Matthew museum, excavations (Mátyás-Király-Múzeum), Fö út 29, ☎ 398126, Open: May-Oct, Tues-Sun 9-16:30, Nov-April, Tues-Sun 8-15:30.

🏰 Royal palace, Fö út 9. Open: Jan-Dec, Tues-Sun, 9-17. 600 meters long and 300 meters wide complex on four terraces. The Lion's fountain of red marble is especially impressive.

🏰 Castle, Open: 16 March-15 Nov, Mon-Sun 9:30-17, 16 Nov-15 March, Mon-Sun 9:30-16. Built in the 13th century. Includes medieval torture chamber. The citadel was the seat of Hungarian kings in the 14th century.

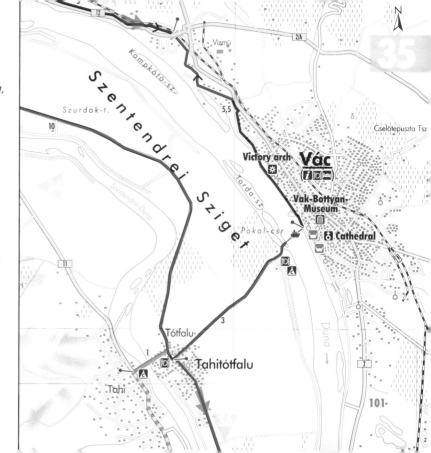

- ❇ **Salomon tower** (Salomon torony), Salomon Torony Street, ✆ 398233, Open: May-Oct, Tues-Sun 9-17. The rooftop terrace offers fine views of both banks of the Danube. Tower contains local history exhibitions with original finds and objects from 3500 BC to the 17th century AD.
- ❇ **Summer toboggan run** (Nyári Bob Pólya), Panoramastraße, Open: April-Sept, holidays only 10-17, Oct-March, holidays only 11-16.
- ❇ **Medieval games in the lower castle** (Salomon tower). A medieval performance by the St. George order of knights presented several times each week. Starts 12:15. The audience is invited to participate in the 90 minute presentation.
- ✉ **Thermal baths** in the Lepence valley, No. 11 main road, (2 kilometers upstream from Visegrád). Open: May-Aug 9-18:30.

Visegrád lies directly on the Danube's "knee" – the narrow gap where the river breaks through the Visegrád mountains and the Börszöny mountains.

Visegrád has played an important strategic role in the region since the first century after Christ, when the Roman Emperor Trajan began building the "limes", the military fortifications that ran along the right bank of the Danube and marked the border of the Roman province Pan-

Danube near Visegrad

nonia. The defenses protected the border as well as roads and rivers that the Romans used. In the 4th century the Romans built a fortress on the 180-meters high Sibirik Hill. This later became the castle that local lords expanded with an irregular ground-plan, thick walls and horseshoe-shaped towers.

In the 10th century Visegrád emerged as a center of local government, joining Esztergom and Buda as one of the early bases of royal and church authority.

In medieval times Hungarian rulers extended the fortifications to defend the land against tribes from the east. The lower castle was built in the 13th century during the Mongol invasions.

In 1246 King Béla IV began construction of the upper castle on the 350-meters high mountain top, to protect surrounding holdings and a convent on what is today known as Margaret Island near Budapest. The island is named after Princess Margaret, who was raised at the convent.

For many years the king's holy crown was kept in the upper castle. When King Albert of Habsburg died in 1439 after a short reign, his wife, Queen Erzsébet (Elisabeth) ordered the theft of the crown. At the time she was pregnant. Her doctors predicted the child would be a boy, and the queen hoped possession of the crown would strengthen her son's claim to the throne. The crown was not returned to Hungary until 20 years later.

The fortifications were then further improved to include an outer wall which extended from the upper castle to the lower castle and down to the banks of the Danube. Parts of this wall still survive today.

Upper castle, Visegrad

After the Turkish occupation the lower castle was neglected and fell into disrepair. In 1871 the main keep was restored and the castle was converted into a royal hunting lodge.

In 1323 the royal court from Temesvár (in what is Romania today) relocated to Visegrád, which temporarily became the king's residence and the Hungarian capital. Initially members of the royal court lived in the castle until construction of the royal palace began at the foot of the mountain. This residence was built on four terraces carved from the side of the slope, and was intended to be the most magnificent Hungarian architectural accomplishment, a monument to the Hungarian Kings' power and wealth. Even after the royal court moved its capital to Buda, the palace in Visegrád remained an important summer residence. During the renaissance King Matthew Corvinus gave the palace its final touches, which contemporary witnesses richly praised.

For many years those testimonials of the palace's beauty were all that remained – it wasn't until 1935 that the ruins of the palace were rediscovered.

Not only the Hungarian kings liked this region. The Turks also remained here for a long period after their 16th century conquests. According to legend, in the year 1570 there was not a single Hungarian person still alive in Visegrád, which was then populated only by Muslims and Greek-Orthodox Bosnians. It was not until 1686 that Visegrád and Buda were liberated from the Turks

Visegrad

and the re-population of the region could begin. Many of the new settlers were Germans, who outnumbered Hungarians and Slavs.

The right bank
from Visegrad to Tahitótfalu   14 km

Continue on Fö út ~ until you reach the B 11 again ~ and turn right onto the main road ~ take the No. 11 main road for another 2.5 kilometers after Visegrád and then the ferry across the smaller arm of the Danube to Kisoroszi.

Tip: The ferry is almost impossible to miss. There is a large sign with the word "rév" at the fish restaurant. The crossing takes just a few minutes.

Kisoroszi
⛴ Ferry to Kisoroszi, 6:30-21:30 hourly, continuous departures every 20-40 minutes.

In Kisoroszi ride about 100 meters down a narrow **103**

street to the main road ∼ turn right towards Tahitótfalu.

Tahitótfalu

Arriving in **Tahitótfalu**, ride to a square with a monument, where the right-bank route converges with the left-bank route coming from **Vác**.

Tip: Here you have two options: Either take the alternative route via Leányfalu or stay on the main route straight ahead towards Szigetmonostor.

Leányfalu route   9 km

From the square with the monument, ride a short distance back towards Kisoroszi and turn left and over a bridge to the other part of Tahitótfalu.

Turn left at the **B 11** ∼ and proceed straight on the main road ∼ a bicycle path begins on the left side near Leányfalu ∼ and soon you come to the landing where the ferry to Szigetmonostor docks.

Tahitótfalu to Szentendre   14 km

To stay on the main route, from the square ride straight on **Becè ut.** ∼ straight ahead ∼ left past Pocsmegyer ∼ towards **Szigetmonostor**.

Szigetmonostor

⛴ **Ferry across the** Szentendrei Duna to „North Szentendre," Határcsárda rév, ✆ 20/9122952. Open between 7:20-20:40, continuous operation.

The posted Danube bicycle route to Szentendre runs right past the ferry landing ∼ take the bicycle path straight until it comes to one of the town's streets ∼ turn left ∼ there is a campground here ∼ soon a bicycle path begins on the left side ∼ and you roll into Szentendre.

Tip: Travelers who have time may wish to make a side trip to the open-air museum (Skanzen), in which accurate replicas of various kinds of Hungarian villages have been built. The museum is about 3 kilometers outside Szentendre and can be reached by following Szabadság-Forrás from the main road.

Skanzen

The term "Skanzen" means open-air museum. The name is actually Swedish – the first museum of this kind was built in 1891 in Stockholm, and was named after the district in which it was established. The name was adopted internationally and is now used in many languages. The idea of an open-air Hungarian exhibition was conceived in 1873 during the Vienna World Fair, where Hungarian houses had been built for an international village. Several years later an ethnographic village was built as part of Hungary's millenium celebrations. Half

Danube "knee"

a year later most of those houses were dismantled.

The open-air museum in Szentendre was established in 1967 and is one of five such sites, where rural architecture and lifestyles are preserved and on display.

Original buildings and objects have been used in an attempt to make the replica villages as authentic as possible. A pond and a stream with several bridges complement the exhibition. There is also a cemetery that shows different methods of interment.

The structures are clustered in ten village-like groups, reflecting the origins of the different kinds of

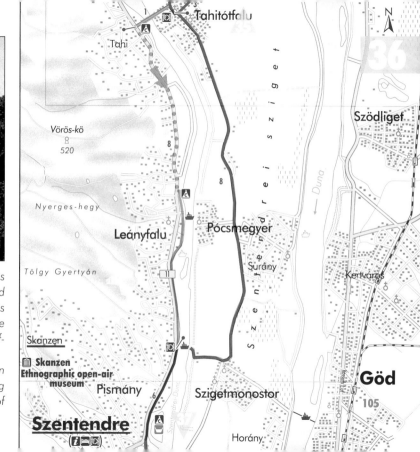

buildings and the regions in which they are most common. Since 1972 the museum has been an independent entity and research center. It also has an extensive ethnographic library with a wealth of materials about Hungarian folk architecture, including drawings, old maps and other documents.

This unique museum is well-worth a visit.

After 400 meters on the No. 11 national road, turn left to get away from the traffic.

Tip: There is a sidewalk along the road which may be used to avoid the perils of the busy No. 11.

The street is named **Ady Endre út** and it divides into two after a couple of hundred meters ～ the street on the left, **Somogyi-Bacsó Part**, is a quay along the Danube and leads past the center of **Szentendre**.

Tip: Downstream from Szentendre the Danube bicycle route on the right bank is posted with signs.

Szentendre
Postal code: 2000; Phone area code: 26
🛈 Tourinform, Dumtsa Jenő u.22, ☎ 317-965

🏛 **"Skanzen" ethnographic open-air museum**, Sztaravodai út, 3 km northwest of town, ☎ 502500 or 502501, Open: April-Oct, Tues-Sun 9-17, July-Aug, 9-19. The museum consists of about 300 authentic replicas of buildings illustrating Hungarian rural living and customs from the 18th and 19th centuries.

🏛 **Margit Kovács collection**, Vastagh Gy. u. 1, ☎ 310244, Open: Jan-14 March, Tues-Sun 10-16, 15 March-Oct, Mon-Sun 10-18, Nov-Dec, Tues-Sun 10-16. Baroque residence from 1750 dedicated to artworks by the Szentendre ceramics maker (1902-77). Her famous figures were often derived from biblical scenes.

🏛 **Szentendre gallery** (Képtár), Fö tér 2-5, Open: April-Oct, Weds-Sun 10-18. Rotating exhibitions of contemporary art.

🏛 **Ferenczy museum**, Fö tér 6, ☎ 310244, Open: April-Oct, Tues-Sun 10-18. Works by members of the Ferenczy family. Károly Ferenczy was a well-known impressionist painter in the late 19th century. His son Béni was a sculptor, daughter Noémi made tapestries.

🏛 **Béla Czóbel museum**, Templom tér 1, Open: April-Oct, 10-18. Collection of works by the expressionist Bela Czóbel (1883-1976), whose early works were strongly influenced by fauvism.

🏛 **Lajos Vajda memorial museum**, Hunyadi u. 1, Open: April-Oct, Tues-Sun 10-18. The body of works by Lajos Vajda (1908-41) reflect the disillusionment of Hungary between the world wars.

🕍 Church of Mary's Annunciation, Fö tér. Greek-orthodox church built by Andreas Mayerhoffer in 1752, as a Serbian Blagovestenska church. Interior includes a beautiful iconostatis from 1790.

🕍 Church of Mary's Ascension, Alkotmány utca. Also called the "Belgrade Cathedral", this Serbian orthodox church was built between 1756 and 1764 and includes a carved icon wall from 1780.

📧 **Public beach** on the Pap-Sziget, Mènèsz u. 3, ☎ 310-697

As in the region around Tata, excavations near Szentendre have also revealed traces of Stone Age settlements that date back about 20,000 years. In the first century after Christ, the Romans established a military camp on the site of the city.

Centuries later it was the Turks who conquered the city and drove the Hungarian population away. After the Turks retreated, many Serbian and Dalmatian immigrants moved to the city, which they called Sveti Andrej (St. Andreas).

Since the 1920s Szentendre has been home to an active colony of artists who live and work in the city and are responsible for numerous galleries, exhibitions and cultural events. This artists community and the city's dominant baroque style contribute to Szentendre's special atmosphere.

A popular destination for tourists is Marx tér, a square at the center of which stands the Memorial Cross erected in 1763 in gratitude for the end of a deadly epidemic. The square is lined with many fine houses built in baroque, rococo and the plain styles of the 17th and 18th centuries. The castle stairs, or Vár-Lépcsö,

lead from the square up to Templom tér (church square) on Church Hill, where one can enjoy excellent views over the roofs of Szentendre and on down to the Danube.

The 15th century church was repeatedly plundered, destroyed and re-built. During renovations after World War II workers discovered Gothic and Romanesque remains, windows and a sun-dial. These can be seen in the church today.

To explore the historic center of Szentendre it is best to lock one's bicycle and go by foot. Many of the streets are paved with rough cobblestones, and the city is also crowded with tourists, restaurants and souvenir stores. There is even a "Folk Art Center."

Szentendre to Budapest   19.5 km

This is now the **Dunakorzó** ~ cross a small bridge ~ stay left just before you reach the intersection with the traffic light ~ ride down **Pannónia ut.** ~ At the end of the street turn right on **Telep ut.** ~ and back to the main road, which has a bicycle path on the left

On the Szentendre-Sziget

side ~ at the junction of the road to **Pomáz**, bicyclists must switch to the right side of the road ~ onto the bicycle path that runs parallel to the main national road ~ you come to an underpass ~ go through it ~ and through a small park ~ and again parallel to the road ~ through another underpass ~ on the left hand you pass a neighborhood of high-rise apartment blocks ~ and arrive at a main intersection near the **Békásmegyer commuter train station.**

Tip: The train station offers an opportunity to take the "Hév" commuter train into the city. Bicycles may be carried on the first and

Open-air museum (Skanzen)

last wagons of the trains; passengers must purchase an extra ticket for their bicycle.

At the **Batthyány tér** station one can switch to the subway towards the main train station (Keleti pu). According to subway baggage regulations, passengers are not allowed to bring bicycles on the subways. A small fine will be collected from passengers caught violating the rule.

If you prefer to ride the bicycle into Budapest, then turn left at the intersection ～ on the right side there is a pedestrian and bicycle path～ but it ends soon and you must ride with traffic ～ to the next section of bicycle path, on the right ～ which ends at another main street ～ proceed to the dam ～ and turn right ～ take the bicycle path away from the road and down towards the Danube ～ at the river the bicycle path turns right and proceeds through residential neighborhoods along the river ～ past beaches, campgrounds, hotels and inns until you reach the railroad.

Turn right along the railroad, cross a stream and ride through the underpass under the railroad ～ go right ～ then continue straight ahead ～ follow the street as it curves to the left ～ and come to an intersection ～ which is somewhat confusing ～ you turn right for a short distance ～ then cross the street on a bicycle path which goes along the right side of the main street ～ the Aquincum museum is at this intersection.

Museum Aquincum

The Romans conquered what is today western Hungary around the time when Christ was born. It became the Province of Pannonia, which was split in two in the second century

Szentendre market square

after Christ. The capital of Lower Pannonia was Aquincum, a settlement in what is today Obuda, the northern part of Budapest. The world Aquincum is derived from the Celtic "Ak Ink" which means roughly "plenty of water."

Ruins of this ancient settlement can still be seen from the main road between Budapest and Szentendre. Even by today's standards, the Roman homes were relatively comfortable, with running water and waste-water lines.

Initially there was just a small Roman force in Aquincum, but by the end of the first century after Christ an entire legion was based here. The first provincial governor to make the city his capital was the future Emperor Hadrian, who moved to Aquincum at the beginning of the second century. Archaeologists have located the governor's palace on the Obudai-sziget. Other ruins of the city, the "municipium" where the civilian population lived, can be seen at the Aquinas museum.

In addition to the Roman city, there was a settlement of Avars with a cult center at the foot of the Gellerthegy. These three communities – the Avar settlement, the Roman military camp, and the civilian Roman city – form what is today known as Aquincum.

The city thrived in the 2nd and 3rd centuries, but by the end of the 4th century the Romans' military strength was sapped and Aquincum was vulnerable to attacks by the nomadic tribes moving into Europe from the east. The Romans evacuated the city in the early 5th century, as part of a deal with the invading Huns.

The remains of the city and its treasures were only uncovered when organized excavations were started in the late 19th century. One of the most valuable finds is a small water-organ of a type that Ktesibius the Greek invented about 140 BC. Science had known of this device from ancient descriptions by the Greek mathematician and mechanic Heron of Alexandria, and from images preserved on ancient coins, but no one had ever heard the instrument's sound. The organ at Aquincum was found in the ruins of a burned house. The 52 bronze whistles produce tones reminiscent of pan-pipes. Among other interesting finds are mosaics in what is known as the Hercules villa

At the Museum Aquincum continue straight ahead ~ along a

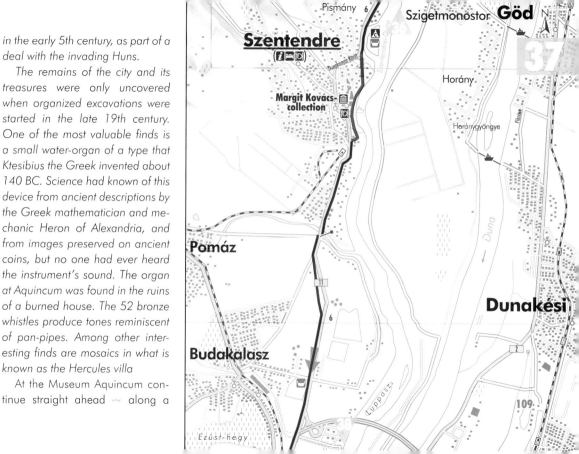

noise barrier ∼ at the end of this barrier turn right ∼ a bicycle and pedestrian path starts on the right side ∼ you ride directly to the right of the railroad ∼ to a street ∼ ahead you should be able to see an industrial lot with a smokestack ∼ turn right at this point ∼ and ride along the wall ∼ the bicycle path is marked with yellow on the pavement ∼ turn right ∼ continue straight ahead ∼ and turn left at the first opportunity ∼ then straight ∼ come to an intersection ∼ continue straight ∼ a bicycle and pedestrian path starts on the right, just before the road cuves to the left ∼ ride through a small park ∼ straight ∼ and down a cobbled path.

Ride up to a small square ∼ where you can see four life-sized bronze figures ∼ stay to the right on this square ∼ and you quickly come to a larger, more romantic square, the Fö tér ∼ straight across the square ∼ to a bus stop ∼ stay left ∼ a bicycle path resumes right before **Árpád híd**.

Tip: Here you can ride up on Árpád híd and continue through the Margit Sziget (a small paradise in the middle of the big city). It takes

you to Margit hid, where you turn right and back on to the main route.

To stay on the main route, ride under the bridge ∼ you should see a green bicycle route sign pointing to **Margit híd** 3 kilometers away ∼ straight ahead ∼ take the bicycle path on the right side ∼ past a small park ∼ until you reach **Margit híd**.

The route now passes some of the impressive buildings and monuments that distinguish the Hungarian capital ∼ first past the **parliament building** on the other side of the river, then Budapest's imposing **Chain Bridge** comes into view ∼ to the right are the **Fisherman's Bastion**, the **Matthias Church** and the **castle** above the city, the **Hotel Gellért** and the **citadel**.

Tip: Budapest has very few bicycle paths and traffic is heavy, which means sightsee-

ing by bicycle is not advisable. The main train station – Keleti pu. – is in Pest and has trains departing in all directions. The easiest route from the Danube to the train station is across the Elisabeth bridge and up Rákóczy út. Motorized traffic and exhaust fumes are extremely heavy, and bicycles are a rarity. If the road is too busy, one can always ride on the sidewalks, which, in Budapest, are relatively wide.

Budapest
Phone area code: 1
🛈 **Tourinform**, V. Vörösmarty tér/Vigadó u.6., ☎ 4388080.
🛈 **Tourinform** Lisztferenc tér 11, ☎ 3224098.
⚓ **Mahart Passnave GmbH**, Passenger ship line, 1056, Belgrád rakpart, ☎ 4384000
🏛 **Museum Aquincum**, Szentendrei út 139, ☎ 4540438, Open: April, Oct, Tues-Sun 10-17, May-Sept, Tues-Sun 10-18. Monuments, ruins and artifacts (2nd-4th centuries AD) from the Roman city of Aquincum.

- **Hungarian national museum (Magyar Nemzeti Múzeum)**, Múzeum körút 14-16, ✆ 3382122, Open: Jan, Dec, Tues-Sun 10-18. The largest and most prestigious museum in Hungary presents diverse collections about the country's history and people.
- **Creative arts museum (Szépmüvészeti Múzeum)**, Dózsa György út 41, ✆ 3439759 Open: Tues-Sun 10-18. World-famous museum contains the largest collection of Spanish masters (Velazquez, Goya, El Greco) outside Spain. The modern gallery includes works by Monet, Pissarro, Renoir, Cézanne, Gauguin and others. Antiquity collection.
- **City historical museum (Történeti Múzeum)**, Castle palais wing E, ✆ 2257809, Open: 1 March-15 May, Weds-Mon 10-18, 16 May-15 Sept, Mon-Sun 10-18, 16 Sept-31 Oct, Weds-Mon 10-18, 1 Nov –28 Feb, Weds-Mon 10-16. Exhibits covering Romanesque to renaissance periods — not to be missed by anyone interested in the city's history and especially the castle district.
- **Hungarian national gallery (Magyar Nemzeti Galéria)**, Disz tér 17,Castle palais wings B-C-D, ✆ 3757533, Open: Jan, Dec, Tues-Sun 10-18. Collection exhibits works by Hungarian painters from the 15th to 19th centuries. Noteworthy are the late Gothic altar pieces, portraits and landscapes by the painter Mihály Munkácsy (1844-1900) and the works by Hungarian impressionists, including Pál Szinyei Merse and Kosztka Tivadar Csontváry.
- **Ludwig museum, contemporary art**, Buda Palace, György tér 2, ✆ 3759175, Open: Tues-Sun 10-18. Contemporary art collection of Irene and Peter Ludwig, of Cologne, provides an overview of the last 50 years of international art, and the last 10 years of contemporary art in Hungary.

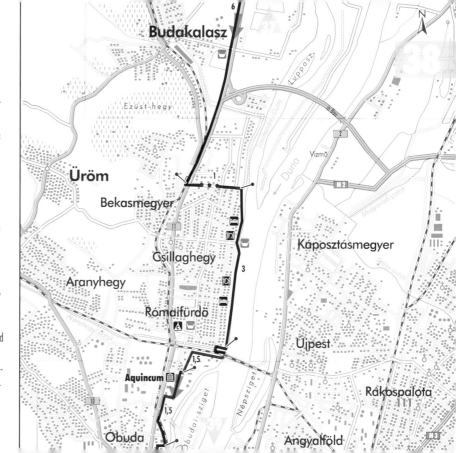

- 🏛 **Museum for applied arts (Iparmüvészeti Múzeum)**, Üllöi út 33-37, ☏ 3759175, Open: Jan, Dec, Tues-Sun 10-18. Wide-ranging collection with household and day-to-day items showing the history of design, housed in a handsome art nouveau building.

- 🏛 **Jewish museum (Zsidó Múzeum)**, Dohány u. 2, ☏ 3428949, Open: Mon-Thurs 10-17, Fri, Sun 10-14. Near the large synagogue, collection with valuable objects of Jewish art, information and exhibits about the deportation of Hungarian Jews during the Nazi period and Nazi concentration camps. In 1993 the museum suffered a major art robbery.

- 🔊 **Vajdahunyad castle**, Városliget. Built between 1896 and 1908 to show the history of Hungarian architecture with examples of different styles, from Romanesque to baroque. Includes a reproduction of Vajdahunyad castle in Transylvania.

- 🔊 **Castle labyrinth**, Úri u. 9, ☏ 212-0287, Open: Mon-Sun 9: 30-19:30. A fascinating presentation of the extensive system of tunnels under the castle, used as storage space in the 16th century, later as a wine cellar. Served as German headquarters during WW2.

- 🔊 **Citadel**, Gellért-Berg. Fortress "guards" the city since 1849, when it was built by the Habsburg rulers in reaction to the Hungarian revolts. Today the hill on which it is built is dominated by the "Liberation Monument," erected in 1947 in

Museum Aquincum

memory of the city's liberation by the Soviet army at the end of WWII. Excellent views of the castle and Budapest

- 🔊 **Great synagogue**, Dohány utca 4. The largest synagogue in Europe, with space for 3,000 people, was built by a student of Otto Wagner. A memorial plaque in memory of Theodor Herzl (born 1860 in Budapest).

- 🔊 **St. Stephan basilica**, Bajcsy-Zsilinszky út. Construction of Budapest's largest church began in 1851. In 1868 the dome collapsed. The eclectic church designed by Miklós Ybl was finally consecrated in 1905.

- ✳ **Castle district**, Buda. This was the center of the medieval city when it was the cultural and political capital of Hungary. After the Turkish occupation, the district was rebuilt in the 18th century.

- ✳ **Margaret island (Margit sziget)**, north of the city. The island's more recent history begins in the late 18th century, when vice-king Joseph von Habsburg built a summer residence and a park with exotic plants and trees. In 1867 mineral springs were discovered, leading to the development of a spa resort. Today closed to motorized traffic, the island is a popular recreation site.

- ✳ **Western train station (Nyugati pu.)**, Teréz körút. Interesting renovated classical terminal train station (1874-77), glass hall by August de Serres and iron construction by Gustave Eiffel, builder of the Eiffel tower in Paris.

- ✳ **Heroes square (Hösök tér)**, Dózsa György út. Square dominated by the millenium monument, built in 1896 for Hungary's 1,000-year celebrations of their conquest of the country, in honor of Hungarian national heroes.

- ✳ **Jewish quarter**, between Dohány u.(Károly krt.) Király u. Kertész u., Rudasbad, Döbrentei tér 9. Before WWII, about 200,000 Jews lived in Budapest. Today about 80,000 live in the city, giving Budapest the largest Jewish population in eastern Europe.

- ✳ **Kiraly baths** (Királyfürdö), Fö utca 84, ☏ 2023688. Turkish bath built 1566 by the Pascha Sokoli Mustafa is one of numerous charming bathhouses and spas in the city. Expanded in the 18th century (baroque) and again in 1827 (classical style). The original pools and dome were retained.

❎ **Rudas baths** (Rudasfürdö), Gellért rakpart, ☎ 3561322. Site of a bathhouse which predated the Turkish bath built in 1566. Fed by radioactive and sulfur waters. Expanded in the late 19th century by Miklós Ybl.

❎ **Old metro** (Földalatti). The oldest underground railroad in Europe, built for the millenium celebrations in 1896, it runs underneath the handsome Andrássy út avenue connecting the central Vörösmarthy tér with the old Zoo in the city park.

❎ **Café Gerbaud**, Vörösmarthy tér. The Budapest coffeehouse most popular among tourists, worth visiting mainly for its elaborate interior.

❎ **Szemlö cave**, Pusztaszeri út 35, ☎ 3256001, Open: Mon, Weds, Fri 10-15, Sat, Sun 10-16. Known as the "underground gardens of Budapest," Eocene cave system with magnificent stalagmites and stalactites.

❎ **Jánoshegy chair lift**, Zugligeti út 97, ☎ 3943764, Open: April-Sept, 9-17, Oct-March 9:30-16; closed Mondays of odd-numbered weeks. Total elevation difference is 262 meters. The lift covers a distance of about one kilometer and runs about 8 meters above the ground. The ride takes about 15 minutes and offers unforgettable views.

❎ **Széchenyi mountain train**, station at Budapest Hotel near Moszkvatér. Built 1874, the 3.5 kilometer cog wheel train goes through Buda's villa district on its way up to Szechenyi mountain.

❎ **Cable car to the castle palace**, Clark Ádám tér, Open: Mon-Sun 7:30-22:00, closed Mondays of even-numbered weeks. Built 1870, historic cable car service brings passengers up to the castle in a few minutes. At the base station, near Chain Bridge, is located the "0-kilometer" stone, from which all distances to Budapest are measured.

🚲 **Bringóhintó**, Margitsziget Hajós Alfred

Budapest

sétány 1, ☎ 3292073
- László Cserny, II, Zuhatag sor 12, ☎ 2006837
- József Fülöp, XIV, Gvadányi u., III, ☎ 2212192
- Rákoskert Bike Center, XVII, Kísérö u. 4, ☎ 2585906

Budapest! One of Europe's great cities – a capital for politics, culture and history, a city that inevitably overwhelms visitors with its majesty and elegance. It is also a city of contrasts and opposites, as well as a young city that has existed in its present form only for just over a century, yet which still exudes the faded glory of its imperial past. As the former sister city to Vienna, and one of the two poles around which the Austro-Hungarian Empire revolved,

Budapest today is proud to be at the middle of a nation that was one of first to cast aside the communist system under which it was governed for most of five decades after WWII.

Budapest is the undisputed queen among Hungarian cities. Many regard it to be among the most beautiful cities in the world. Few other cities have so well understood how to wrap themselves in an aura of festiveness and brilliance.

The first people were drawn to this fertile land in prehistoric times, attracted by the shimmering waters of the river and the plain spreading eastward from the mountains. Two-thousand years ago the Romans established a city on the west bank. Legally speaking, the city of Budapest was born in 1873, when the towns of Pest, Buda and Obuda were merged. But the roots of Budapest go back to Illyrian-Celtic Avars and the Romans who lived in Aquincum.

The Magyars then built the Kurszans castle, their first center of authority. In 1241 the Mongols destroyed Buda and Pest. In 1247 King Béla IV built the first royal castle on castle hill

Budapest

– it soon became his permanent residence. He awarded city rights to Pest, including the stone quarry and Little Pest on the left bank of the Danube. The name Pest seems to come from the old Slavic word for oven (pesti), referring to the ovens used to treat chalk.

After the Turks conquered Hungary, Budapest became the provincial capital for a Pasha. Many of the bath-houses left by the Romans were rebuilt in this period as Turkish baths. After the Turks were expelled in the late 17th century, the city began to experience a new economic and cultural boom. By 1848 the traditional main city of Buda had been overtaken by Pest

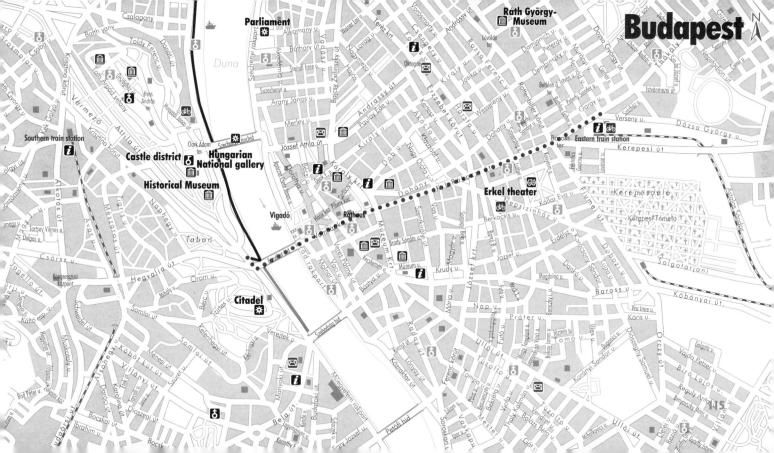

Budapest

Parliament

Ráth György-Museum

Southern train station

Castle district

Hungarian National gallery

Historical Museum

Vigadó

Rathaus

Citadel

Erkel theater

Eastern train station

115

as the spiritual and political center of the country. During this period the city was seized by the trend toward modernity. In 1896 Budapest became the second city in the world, after London, to open a subway. Many of the city's iron and glass train stations and market buildings were built in this period.

The wide and lazy Danube through the center of the city played a key role in every part of Budapest's history. Today 8 bridges connect the two halves of the city, and the river remains central to Budapest's character, the unifying element that make Buda, Pest and the river's islands into a harmonious whole.

Buda is the older part of the city, but its lively center today is located in Pest.

Among the many architectural edifices that dot the cityscape with a variety of styles, one

Fisherman's Bastion

of the most distinctive is the Fisherman's Bastion in the old Castle District. Behind it stands the distinguished old Matthias church and the old city hall with its renaissance windows. The Castle District is a dense maze of small streets and alleys, where handsome baroque city palaces stand next to old patrician houses, some of which are built on Gothic foundations.

Above the city on Castle Mountain stands the royal palace. It was heavily damaged by fire when the Ottoman Turks withdrew from the city. Franz A. Hillebrand rebuilt it in the baroque style, and it was later rebuilt by Miklós Ybl. In 1945 it burned again. Visitors to the Castle District should not neglect a visit at Uri utca 9. It is the entrance to a 10-kilometer network of natural caves and man-made connecting tunnels that honeycombs the mountain

Parliament in Budapest

beneath the castle. Many of the tunnels date back to late medieval times.

As people who enjoy bicycle trips and touring, the bikeline team is happy and proud that you have chosen this book to guide you on your adventure along the Danube River. We sincerely hope you have found it to be informative, accurate and easy to use. We also hope that select other books from our bikeline, cycline or skateline series the next time you are planning a travelling vacation.

Overnight accommodations

The following list includes hotels (H), hotels garni (Hg), inns (Gh), pensions (P), private rooms/farm (Pz/Bh) and vacation apartments (FW) as well as youth hostels and campgrounds in the towns along the cycle route. These towns are not listed in alphabetical order, but according to their location along the river.

We have not attempted to list every possible place where visitors can spend the night, and listings should not be construed as any kind of recommendation. The Roman number (I-VI) after the telephone number indicates price range. These fall into six categories, listed below, and do not necessarily reflect the relative comfort and quality available:

1 €	=		246,– HUF
	=		39,– SKK
I	under € 15,–		
	HUF 3.690,– / SKK 585,–		
II	€ 15,–	to	€ 23,–
	HUF 3.690,–	to	HUF 5.658,–
	SKK 585,–	to	SKK 897,–
III	€ 23,–	to	€ 30,–
	HUF 5.658,–	to	HUF 7.380,–
	SKK 897,–	to	SKK 1.170,–
IV	€ 30,–	to	€ 35,–
	HUF 7.380,–	to	HUF 8.610,–
	SKK 1.170,–	to	SKK 1.365,–
V	€ 35,–	to	€ 50,–
	HUF 8.610,–	to	HUF 12.300,–
	SKK 1.365,–	to	SKK 1.950,–
VI	over € 50,–		
	HUF 12.300,– / SKK 1.950,–		

These categories are based on the price per person in a double room equipped with shower or bath, with breakfast, unless otherwise indicated. Rooms with bath or shower in the hall are indicated with the symbol ⚼.

Because we wish to expand this list and keep it up-to-date, we welcome any comments, additions or corrections you may have. There is no charge for a listing.

Vienna (A)

Postal code: 1xx0 (xx = Bezirk); Phone area code: 01

🛈 Wien-Tourismus, ✆ 24555

1. Bezirk:

H De France, Schottenring 3, ✆ 313680, VI
H Vienna Marriott, Parkring 12a, ✆ 51518-0, VI
H Austria, Wolfeng. 3/Fleischmarkt 20, ✆ 51523, VI
H Kärntnerhof, Grashofg. 4, ✆ 5121923, V-VI

H Römischer Kaiser, Annag. 16, ☎ 5127751-0, VI
H König von Ungarn, Schulerstr. 10, ☎ 515840, VI
H Post, Fleischmarkt 24, ☎ 515830, V-VI
H Schweizerhof, Bauernmarkt 22, ☎ 5331931, V-VI
H Tigra, Tiefer Graben 18, ☎ 5339641, VI
H Zur Wiener Staatsoper, Krugerstr. 11, ☎ 5131274, VI
P Dr. Geissler, Postg. 14, ☎ 5332803, III-V
P Residenz, Ebendorferstr. 10, ☎ 40647860, V
P Christina, Hafnersteig 7, ☎ 5332961, V-VI
P Riedl, Georg-Coch-Pl. 3/4/10, ☎ 5127919, V

P Sacher Apartm., Rotenturmstr. 1, ☎ 5333238, V-VI
P Schweizer, Heinrichsg. 2, ☎ 5338156, V
P Aviano, Marco d'Avianog. 1, 5128830, V-VI

2. Bezirk:

H City-Central, Taborstr. 8a, ☎ 21105, VI
H Lassalle, Engerthstr. 173-175, ☎ 213150, VI
H Adlon, Hofenederg. 4, ☎ 2166788, V
H Capri, Praterstr. 44-46, ☎ 2148404, V-VI
H Cristall, Franzensbrückenstr. 9, ☎ 2168142, V-VI
H Holiday Inn Vienna, Handelskai 269, ☎ 72777, VI

H Nordbahn, Praterstr. 72, ☎ 21130-0, V-VI
H Stefanie, Taborstr. 12, ☎ 21150-0, VI
H Vienna, Grosse Stadtgutg. 31, ☎ 2143317 od. 2, V-VI
H Wilhelmshof, Kleine Stadtgutg. 4, ☎ 2145521, V-VI
H Stadt Brünn, Rotensterng. 7a, ☎ 2146322, V
H Franzenshof, Große Stadtgutg. 19, ☎ 2166282 od. 21662, III-IV
H Praterstern, Mayerg. 6, ☎ 2140123, III
P Vienna City Appartements, Darwing. 8/18, ☎ 0699/19259421, V-VI

3. Bezirk:

H Im Palais Schwarzenberg, Schwarzenbergpl. 9, ☎ 7984515, VI
H Roter Hahn Tourotel, Landstr. Hauptstr. 40, ☎ 7132568-0, V-VI
H Biedermeier, Landstrasser Hauptstr. 28, ☎ 71671-0, VI
H Urania, Obere Weißgerberstr. 7, ☎ 7131711, IV-VI
H Gartenhotel Gabriel, Landstrasser Hauptstr. 165, ☎ 7123205, IV-V
H Goldene Spinne, Linke Bahng. 1a, ☎ 7124486, V
H Urania, Obere Weissgerberstr. 7, ☎ 7131711, IV-VI
H Don Bosco, Hagenmüllerg. 33, ☎ 71184555, III
P Bosch, Keilg. 13 (nähe Südbhf.), ☎ 7986179, IV-V
P Kirchbichler, Landstrasser Hauptstr. 33, ☎ 7121068, III-IV

4. Bezirk:

H Clima Hotel Johann Strauss, Favoritenstr. 12, ☎ 5057624, VI
H Prinz-Eugen, Wiedner Gürtel 14, ☎ 5051741, VI
H Ho. Inn Wien City, Margarethenstr. 53, ☎ 58850, VI
H Beim Theresianum, Favoritenstr. 52, ☎ 5051606, V-VI

H Carlton Opera, Schikaneder g. 4, ☎ 5875302, V-VI
H Congress, Wiedner Gürtel 34, ☎ 5055506, V-VI
H Drei Kronen, Schleifmühlg. 25, ☎ 5873289, IV
H Margareten, Margaretenstr. 30, ☎ 588150, III-V

5. Bezirk:

H Art Hotel Vienna, Brandmayerg. 7-9, ☎ 54451080, V-VI
H Amarante, Matzleinsdorferpl. 1, ☎ 5442743, VI
H Ananas, Rechte Wienzeile 93-95, ☎ 546200, VI

6. Bezirk:

H President Wallg. 23, ☎ 59990, VI
H Schneider, Getreidemarkt 5, ☎ 588380, VI
H Füger Westend City Hostel, Fügerg. 3, ☎ 59767290, IV
Kolpinghaus-Wien Zentral, Gumpendorferstr. 39, ☎ 5875631, IV-V
P Corvinus, Mariahilferstr. 57-59, ☎ 5877239, IV-V
P Haydn, Mariahilfer Str. 57-59, ☎ 58744140, V
P Esterhazy, Nelkeng. 3, ☎ 5875159, II-III
P Spachta, Gfronerg. 2, ☎ 5970305, IV

7. Bezirk:

H Admiral, Karl-Schweigerhofer-G. 7, ☎ 521410, V-VI
H Kugel, Siebensterng. 43, ☎ 5233355, IV
H Am Brillantengrund, Bandg. 4, ☎ 5233662, VI
H Fürstenhof, Neubaugürtel 4, ☎ 5233267, IV-VI

H K & K Maria Theresia, Kirchbergg. 6-8, ☎ 52123, VI
P Pharmador, Schottenfeldg. 39, ☎ 5235317, VI
P Alla Lenz, Halbg. 3-5, ☎ 52369890, IV-VI
P Carantania, Kandlg. 35, ☎ 5267340, V
P Anna, Zieglerg. 18/1, ☎ 5230106, IV-V
P Atrium, Burggasse 118, ☎ 5233114, III-V
P Minu 3, Neubaug. 11, ☎ 5264652, III-IV
JH, 7, Myrtheng./Neustiftg. 85, ☎ 5236316

8. Bezirk:

H Concordia, Schönborng. 6, ☎ 4011810, VI
H Graf Stadion, Buchfeldg. 5, ☎ 4055284, VI
H Rathaus, Lange G. 13, ☎ 4060123, IV-V

P Andreas, Schlösselg. 11, ☎ 4053488, III-V
P Baronesse, Lange G. 61, ☎ 4051061, V-VI
P Columbia, Kochg. 9, ☎ 40567570, V-VI
P Felicitas, Josefsg. 7, ☎ 4057212, IV
P Baltic, Skodag. 15, ☎ 4056266 III-IV
P Zipser, Lange G. 49, ☎ 404540, V-VI

9. Bezirk:

H Albatros, Liechtensteinstr. 89, ☎ 3173508, VI
H Arkadenhof, Viriotg. 5, ☎ 3100837, VI
H Bellevue, Althanstr. 5, ☎ 313480, VI
H Atlanta, Währinger Str. 33, ☎ 4051239, V-VI
H Harmonie, Harmonieg. 5-7, ☎ 3176604, VI

H Mozart, Nordbergstr. 4, (Nähe Donaukanal) ☎ 3171537, IV-VI
H Strudlhof, Pasteurg.1, ☎ 3192522, VI
P Appartm. 700m zum Ring, Van-Swieten-G. 8, ☎ 40936800, V
P Bleckmann, Währinger Str. 15, ☎ 4080899, V
P Franz, Währinger Str. 12, ☎ 31040400, V
P Auer, Lazarettg. 3, ☎ 4062121 od. 4067103, III
P Samwald, Hörlg. 4, ☎ 3177407, III
P Astra, Alserstr. 32, ☎ 4024354, IV-V
P Appartement Wien Central, Sechsschimmelg. 4/17, ☎ 0664/1616331

10. Bezirk:

H Bosei, Gutheil-Schoderg. 9, ✆ 66106, VI

H/P Cyrus, Laxenburger Str. 14, ✆ 6022578, IV

H Schweizerhof, Bauernmarkt 22, ✆ 5331931, VI

P Am Kurpark, Burgenlandg. 72, ✆ 6884508, IV-V

P Puzwidu, Himberger Str. 69, ✆ 6882168, IV-V

P Wildenauer, Quellenstr. 120, ✆ 6042153, IV

11. Bezirk:

H Weber, Kaiser-Ebersdorfer-Str. 283-285,
✆ 7696973, V

P Czeczil, Zinnerg. 42, ✆ 0664/1075969, V

12. Bezirk:

H Altmannsdorf, Hoffingerg. 26-28, ✆ 801230, VI

H Cryston, Gaudenzdorfer Gürtel 63, ✆ 8135682,
V-VI

H Bergwirt, Maxingstr. 76, ✆ 8773413, V-VI

Gh Riede, Niederhofstr. 18, ✆ 8138576, IV

🏠 Jugendgästehaus Kolpingfamilie, Bendlg. 10-
12, ✆ 8135487

13. Bezirk:

H Cortina, Hietzinger Hauptstr. 134, ✆ 87774060,
V-VI

H Auhof, Auhofstr. 205, ✆ 8775289, II

Gh Schneider-Gössl, Firmiang. 9-11, ✆ 8776109, V

14. Bezirk:

H Kavalier, Linzer Str. 165, ✆ 910020, VI

H Rustler, Linzer Str. 43, ✆ 9820162, V

H Matauschek, Breitenseer Str. 14, ✆ 9823532, IV

P Rosengarten, Underreing. 33-35, ✆ 91452800,
V

P Anzengruber, Anzengruberstr. 59, ✆ 9792214, III-
IV

P Pillmeier, Sofienalpenstr. 9, ✆ 9792183, III-IV

P Voggeneder, Josef-Palme-Pl. 3, ✆ 9791207, VI

🏠 Jugendgästehaus Hütteldorf-Hacking, Schloss-
bergg. 8, ✆ 8771501

🅰 Wien-West I, Hüttelbergstr. 40 (U4 bis Hüt-
teldorf), ✆ 941449, 15. Juli-28. Aug.

🅰 Wien-West II, Hüttelbergstr. 80, ✆ 9142314

15. Bezirk:

H Reither, Graumanng. 16, ✆ 8936841, VI

H Lucia, Hütteldorfer Str. 79, ✆ 78652720, V

H Zur Stadthalle, Hackeng. 20 (Westbhf), ✆ 9824272,
V-VI

H Westbahn, Pelzg. 1, ✆ 9821480, V-VI

H Altwienerhof, Herklotzg. 6, ✆ 8926000, V-VI

P Zur Stadthalle, Hackeng. 33, ✆ 9824272, IV-V

P Fünfhaus, Sperrg. 12, ✆ 8923545, III

P Mailberg, Holocherg. 17, ✆ 9835634, II

16. Bezirk:

H Gallitzinberg, Johann-Staud-Str. 32,
✆ 4198770, V

H Zur Schwalbe, Degeng. 45, ✆ 4861181, V-VI

H Hadrigan, Maroltingerg. 68, ✆ 4932062, IV-V

H Thalia, Lindauerg. 2-6, ✆ 4054513, IV

P Moser, Maroltingerg. 73, ✆ 4939173, IV

🏠 Schlossherberge am Wilhelminenberg, 16, Sa-
voyenstr. 2, ✆ 4858503-700

17. Bezirk:

H Stahlehner, Ranftlg. 11, ✆ 4082505, III-IV

H Jäger, Hernalser Hauptstr. 187, ✆ 48666200, VI

H Maté, Ottakringer Str. 34-36, ☎ 40455, VI

H Maté-Dependance, Bergsteigg. 22, ☎ 40466, V-VI

P Appartments Bernhofer, Haslingerg. 74, ☎ 4810441, III-V

P Haus Neuwaldegg, Neuwaldegger Str. 23, ☎ 4863396, III

P Appartm. Bernhofer, Haslingerg. 74, ☎ 4810441, III-V

18. Bezirk:

H Thüringer Hof, Jörgerstr. 4-8, ☎ 401790, V-VI

H Faist, Schulg. 9, ☎ 4062405, III-IV

19. Bezirk:

H Clima Villenhotel, Nussbergg. 2c, ☎ 371516, VI

H Glanzing, Glanzingg. 23, ☎ 47042720, VI

H Park-Villa, Hasenauerstr. 12, ☎ 3675700, VI

H Schild, Neustift am Walde 97-99, ☎ 44040440, V-VI

Gh Zur Agnes, Sieveringer Str. 221, ☎ 4401424, IV-V

🏠 Haus Döbling, 19, Gymnasiumstr. 85, ☎ 347631-16, Juli-Sept., I-II

20. Bezirk:

🏠 Jugendgästehaus Brigittenau, 20, Friedrich-Engels-Pl. 24, ☎ 3328294-0

H Ibis Wien, Lassallestr. 7a, ☎ 217700, V

H Vienna, Grosse Stadtgut. 31, ☎ 2143317, V-VI

H Laselle, Engerthstr. 173-175, ☎ 21315, VI

21. Bezirk:

H Karolinenhof, Jedlseer Str. 75, ☎ 2787801, V-VI

H Berger, Brünner Str. 126, ☎ 2921665, V-VI

Gh Strebersdorferhof, Rußbergstr. 46, Strebersdorf, ☎ 2925722, IV

P Dreikellerhof, Strebersdorfer Str. 172, Strebersdorf, ☎ 2925407

22. Bezirk:

H Donauzentrum, Wagramer Str. 83-85, ☎ 2035545, VI

H Hillinger Donaucity, Erzherzog-Karl-Str. 105, ☎ 20446460, V-VI

H Asperner Löwe, Aspernstr. 96, ☎ 2882088, IV

H Forum Wien, Wagramer Str. 21, ☎ 260200, VI

H Landgasthof Müllner, Esslinger Hauptstr. 82, ☎ 7747484, IV

H Alte Donau, Wagramer Str. 51, ☎ 2044094, V

🏠 Neue Donau, Am Kleihäufel, ☎ 2024010

23. Bezirk:

H Stasta, Lehmanng. 11, ☎ 8659788, V

H Hofinger, Schuppeng. 19-21, ☎ 661020, V

P Erlaa, Erlaaer Str. 148, ☎ 6671204, V

P Altmann, Breitenfurter Str. 515, ☎ 8898882, IV

🏕 Schwimmbad-Camping Radaun, An der Au 2 (S-Bahn bis Liesing) ☎ 884154, 25. März-20. Nov.

🏕 Camping Wien Süd, Breitenfurter Str. 269, ☎ 8673649

Orth a. d. Donau (A)

Postal code: 2304; Telephone area code: 02212

ℹ️ Gemeindeamt, Am Markt 26, ☎ 2208

Gh Danubius, Am Markt 6, ☎ 2400, II

Gh Binder, Jägergrund 2, ☎ 2252, I-II

P Marchfelder Pension, Schwarzeckerweg 4, ☎ 3120

P Schlossblick, Hanfgartenweg 10, ☎ 2772

P Maria, Uferstr. 1, ☎ 2843, I-II

Pz Weinstube Zur Alten Schule, Altes Dorf 6, ☎ 2136, II

Pz Zahlbrecht, Jägergrund 5, ☎ 24436, II

Eckartsau (A)

Postal code: 2305; Telephone area code: 02214

ℹ️ Gemeindeamt, Obere Hauptstr. 1, ☎ 2202

Gh Kramreiter, Hauptstr. 12, ☎ 2203, III

Pz Moik, Marktpl. 3, ☎ 2235, II

Pz Kaltenbrunner, Obere Hauptstr. 20, ☎ 2883, II

Engelhartstetten

Postal code: 2292; Telephone area code: 02214

Pz Ornauer, Untere Hauptstr. 5, ☎ 2468

Loimersdorf:

Gh Weber, Ortstr. 61, ☎ 2252

Gh Prinz Eugen, 2294 Schlosshof 60, ☎ 02285/6350

Pz Pekarek, Ortsstr. 58, ☎ 2286

Stopfenreuth

Telephone area code: 02214

Gh Forsthaus Stopfenreuth, Uferstraße 1, ☎ 2232

Bad Deutsch Altenburg (A)

Postal code: 2405; Telephone area code: 02165

🖪 Tourismusbüro, Kurverwaltung Bad Deutsch Altenburg, Erhardg. 2, ☎ 62900

H Kurzentrum Ludwigstorff, Badg. 21, ☎ 626170, III-V

H König Stephan, Badg. 34, ☎ 64711, II-III

Gh Stöckl, Hauptpl. 3, ☎ 62337, III

Gh Zum Amphitheater, Wiener Str. 51, ☎ 62737, II-III

P Bichler, Badg. 38, ☎ 64636, II

P Riedmüller, Badg. 28, ☎ 62473-0, II-III

P Hofmeister, Badg. 7, ☎ 62768, III

P Madle, Badg. 22, ☎ 62763, II

P Schön, Neustiftg. 10. ☎ 62753, II

Petronell-Carnuntum (A)

Postal code: 2404; Telephone area code: 02163

122 🖪 Gemeindeamt, Kirchenpl. 1, ☎ 2228

H Marc-Aurel, Hauptstr. 10, ☎ 2285, IV-V

Gh Zum Heidentor, Hauptstr. 129, ☎ 2201

🅰 Peiritsch, Bruckerstr. 470, ☎ 2989

Hainburg (A)

Postal code: 2410; Telephone area code: 02165

🖪 Gemeindeamt, Hauptpl. 23, ☎ 62111

🖪 Gästeinformation, ☎ 62111-23

Gh „Zum goldenen Anker", Donaulände 27, ☎ 64810, III-V

Gh Pizzeria Slavik, Pressburger Reichsstr. 72, ☎ 64840, II

P Waldgasthaus, Burgenlandstr. 85, ☎ 62549, II

P Schlossblick, ☎ 0676/9454060 od. 62549, II-III

Pz Putz, Schanzstr. 6, ☎ 63956, I 🏠

Pz Obleser, Schönwieserstr. 15, ☎ 0699/11571063, II

Pz Schweiger, Hollitzerallee 28, ☎ 64316, II

Wolfsthal-Berg (A)

Postal code: 2412; Telephone area code: 02165

🖪 Gemeindeamt, ☎ 62676

Pz Korseska, Hauptstr. 39, ☎ 63511, I-II

Bratislava (SK)

Postal code: 82000; Telephone area code: 02

🖪 Bratislava Information Service, Klobučnicka 2, ☎ 54434325

H Adonis, Vicie hrdlo, II

H Astra, Prievozska 14, ☎ 58238111

H Hostel Backpacker's, Panenska 31, II

H Baronka, Mudrochova 2, ☎ 44872324, II

H Borik, Na boriku 15, ☎ 54431583

H Botel Fairway, Nabr. arm. gen. L. Svobodu, III

H Botel Marina, Nabrezie arm. gen. L. Svobodu, IV

H City Bratislava, Seberiniho 9, ☎ 43337980, IV

H Danube, Rybne namestie 1, ☎ 59340000, VI

H Devin, Riecna ul. 4, ☎ 54433640, V-VI

H Dukla, Dulovo 1, ☎ 55969815

H Echo, Presovska 39, ☎ 55569170, II

H Forum, Hodzovo namestie 2, ☎ 59348142, VI

H Holiday Inn, Bajkalska 25A, ☎ 48245121

H No16, Partizanska 16a, ☎ 54411672, VI

H Ibis, Zamocka 38, IV

H Incheba, Viedenska 7, ☎ 67272000

H Junior, Drienova 14, ☎ 43334340

H Kamila, Cierna voda 611, ☎ 45943611, V-VI

H Kyjev, Rajská 2, ☎ 53961082, III-V

H Marrol's, Tobrucka 4, VI

H Medium, Tomasikova 34, III

H Miva, Bzovicka 38, ☎ 63821052, III

H Nivy, Liscie nivy 3, ☎ 55410390

H Perugia, Zelena 5, ☎ 54431824

H Plus, Bulharska 72, ☎ 43294445, I

H Radisson SAS Carlton, Hviezdoslavovo nam. 3, ☎ 59390000, VI

H Rapid, Telocvicna 11, ☎ 43410257, I

H Remy, Stara vajnorska cesta 37a, ☎ 44455063, I

H Sorea, Kralovske udolie 6, ☎ 54414442, II

H Spirit, Vancurova 1, II

H Sportkontakt, Presovska 38, ☎ 44454571

H Tatra, nám. 1. mája 5, ☎ 59272123, V

H Turist, Ondavska 5, ☎ 55572789, II

H UVS, Bardosova 33, ☎ 54772060, II

H West, Koliba-Kamzik, ☎ 54788692, V

P Zvarac, Pionierska 17, ☎ 492467600-1

P Arcus, Moskovska, ☎ 55572522

P Gremium, Gorkeho 11, ☎ 54430653, II

P Chez David, Zamocka 13, ☎ 54416943

P Stevan, Rusovská cesta 22, I-II

P Pegas, Vapenka 15, IV

🏠 Mladá garda, Racianska 103, ☎ 44253065

🏠 Bernolak, Bernolakova 1, ☎ 52497721

🏠 Svoradov, Svoradova 13, ☎ 54411908

🏠 Mladost, Mlynska dolina

🏠 Hostel Gabriel's, Paulinyho 1

P Lindtner, metská élistov 34, ☎ 5626021

Gabčíkovo (SK)

Postal code: 93005

H Arpád, Hlavná 1040

Zlatná na Ostrove (SK)

Telephone area code: 035
P He-Ge, Školská 123, ☎ 7781206
🏠 Sportova hala, Tourist-hostel, ☎ 7793341 od. 7793168.
🅰 Autocamping, summer only

Komárno (SK)

Postal code: 94501; Telephone area code: 035
ℹ️ Touristinformation, Zupna ul. 5, ☎ 730063
H Europa a. s., M.R. Stefánika 1 (Center), ☎ 7731349-50
H Danubius, Dunajské nábrezie, ☎ 7731091
H Čajka, Bratislavska Cesta 2, ☎ 7750208
H Sport Hotel, Velkodunajske Nabrezie 15
H Panoráma, Sportová, ☎ 7713151, or 7713113
P Delta, Malodunajské nábrezie 10, ☎ 7731566
P Carda Apaly, Mrtve Rameno Vahu, V
P Banderium, Nam M.R. Stefanika 11
P Jarka, Platinová 42, ☎ 7731163
P Michaela, Vnútorná Okružná 17/102, ☎ 627465
P Ring Bar, Letná 4, ☎ 7713158

Patince (SK)

Postal code: 94639; Telephone area code: 035
H Partek, Patince, ☎ 7787754
P Pramen, Patrek Organizacia Cestovneho Ruchu, ☎ 98406

P Šport, ☎ 7787767
Pz Chatová osada Family Resort, Patince-Kúpele 147, ☎ 7731444
Pz Ubytovanie v súkromi Padi, ☎ 7787656, oder 0908/136701

Muzla (SK)

Postal code: 94352; Telephone area code: 0036
H Montanara, Muzla 713, ☎ 7583200
Pz Tereza, Muzla 468, ☎ 7583200

Štúrovo (SK)

Postal code: 94301; Telephone area code: 036
H Others Termálne kúpalisko Vadaš TU, Vadašská, ☎ 75111572
H Others Ubytovacie zariadenie Vadaš, Termálne kúpalisko II., ☎ 7511410
H Others Ubytovňa Butik Centrum, Hlavná 7, ☎ 7511312
H Guest Centre, Hlavná 78, ☎ 7511023
H Šport, Športova 5, ☎ 7511035
H Zahovay, Námestie Slobody 10, ☎ 7511137
H Motel Non Stop, Hlavná 34, ☎ 7511410
P KeruVia, Nánanská cesta 63, ☎ 035/6400962
P Mika, Bocskayho 29, ☎ 0905/821594
P St. Florian, Sv. Stefana 41, ☎ 7522067, II-IV
P Atrium, Hlavna 51, ☎ 7512507, II-IV
P Hostel Dunaj, Ostrihomská 6, ☎ 7511036

P Penzión Kormoš, Komenského 8, ☎ 0905/513732, II
🅰 Campsite ATC Vadaš termálne kúpalisko, Vadašská, ☎ 7511410, 7511572

Rajka (H)

Telephone area code: 096
H Rajka, Bem Apó u. 5, ☎ 320667
🅰 Aranykárász Kemping, Mosoni-Dunapart, ☎ 30/2164-122

Dunakiliti (H)

Postal code: 9225; Telephone area code: 96
H Princess Palace, Kossuth u. 117, ☎ 671071, VI
P Géméskut Fogadó, Külterület, ☎ 224065, 671-470 III
P Mkay Apartmanház, Rév u. 70, ☎ 30/247-8830
P Villa Hedi, Gyümölcsös út 58, ☎ 224554
Pz Hoffer, Gyümölcsös u. 28a, ☎ 213562
Pz Öry, Kossuth u. 79b, ☎ 228028
Pz Szedlák, Jószef A.u. 14, ☎ 224559
Pz Makai Vendégház, ☎ 671017
🅰 Vizpart, Kossuth u. 74, ☎ 224579
🅰 Vadvíz Kemping, Duzzasztómü ☎ 30/2172-497, 30/4866-922

Dunasziget (H)

Postal code: 9227; Telephone area code: 096
P Fehér Vendégház, Cikola u. 56, ☎ 233-411, 30/
567-3422
Fw Búroki Vendégház, Doborgaz u. 46, ☎ 233-137
P Dunaszigeti Erdei Iskola, Sérfenyö u. 119, ☎ 20/3562068
P Karolina Apartmanházak, Cikola u. 39a, ☎ 233060, 20/3563-585
P Maywald Vendégház, Sérfenyö u. 119, ☎ 233350, II
P Zátonyi Csárda, Zátonyi u. 3, ☎ 233505
Pz Mofém Pihenöház, Doborgaz u. 22, ☎ 574565
🅰 Kisvesszösi Kemping, Cikola u. 39, ☎ 233060
🅰 Búroki Vendégház, Doborgaz u. 46, ☎ 233137

Dunaremete (H)

Postal code: 9235; Telephone area code: 096
P Platán Étterem, Kossuth L. u. 1/a, ☎ 566090
P Dunaremete, Szabadság u. 2, ☎ 213533

Mosonmagyaróvár (H)

Postal code: 9200; Telephone area code: 96
ℹ️ Tourinform, Kápclna tér 16, ☎ 206304
ℹ️ Ciklámen Tourist, Fö út 8., ☎ 217344
H Panoráma, Frankel Leó u. 21, ☎ 216167, II
H Thermal, Kolbai út 10, ☎ 206871
H Corvina Szálloda, Mosonyi Mihály út 2, ☎ 218131
H Riviéra Bacardi Beach, Strand u., ☎ 206076, 70/2428973

123

H Solaris, Lucsony u. 19, ☎ 215300, II-III

H St. István, Istvánpuszta Pf. 140, ☎ 213011, II-III

H Thermal Hotel, Kolbai út 10, ☎ 206871

H Fészek Fogadò, Kígyó u. 22, ☎ 211599

H Gazdász Szálloda, Gazdász u. 10, ☎ 215444, II

H Easy Life Club, Krisztina major, ☎ 214511

H Fekete Sas, Fö u. 9, ☎ 215842

H Motel Net T, Kölcsey u. 4, ☎ 576796

H Motel Kis-Duna, Gabonarakpart 6, ☎ 216433

P Oroszlán Panzió, Gorkij u. 48, ☎ 213540

P Nimród, Királyhidai út 59, ☎ 211141

P Rósza, Kálnoki u. Pf 69, ☎ 212487

P Sarokház, Szent Istvan u. 99, ☎ 216056

P Solar Appartmanház, Gyümölcsös u. 34, ☎ 215300

P Vitalitas panzió, Kereszt utca 5, ☎ 576754

Pz Kovács, Zurányl u. 3, ☎ 212135, II-III

Pz Pinter Vendeghaz, Fatelep u. 7, ☎ 216141

🅰 Kis-Duna Kemping, Gabonarakpart 6, ☎ 216433

🅰 Napsugar Kemping, Gorkij u. 29a, ☎ 211226

Halászi (H)

Postal code: 9228; Telephone area code: 96

H Babos-Major & Duna Outdoor Center, Halászi Ùgò, 714001

Pz Regia, Kossuth u. 102., ☎ 210684

Fw Radek Vendégház, Kossuth u. 21, ☎ 210436

🅰 Party Csárda, Szabadidöpark és Sátorozóhely, Dunasétány, ☎ 210088

Lipót (H)

Postal code: 9233; Telephone area code: 096

H Orchidea, Rákóczi u. 42-44, ☎ 674042

P Hort Duna, Fö út 65, ☎ 674028

P Fehér Hattyú, Fö út 80, ☎ 216572, I

P Kék Duna, Petöfi S. u. 3, ☎ 674018, 674019

Pz Fazekas, Kossuth u. 27, ☎ 216549

Pz Bogdan, Béke fasor 7, I

🅰 Holt-Duna Kemping, Holt-Duna 1, ☎ 30/9118154

Hédervár (H)

Postal code: 9178; Telephone area code: 096

H Schlosshotel Hédervár, Fö u. 47, ☎ 213433

P Park, Fö út 41, ☎ 719259

P Kont, Kossuth L. u. 13, ☎ 215430

Fw Kék Apartman, Kossuth L. u. 13, ☎ 215430

Ásványráró (H)

Postal code: 9177; Telephone area code: 096

H Öreg Duna Csárda, Györi u. 28, ☎ 704280

P Horgásztanya, Petöfi u. 45, ☎ 524988

P Szürke Gém Fogadó, Rákóczi F. u. 52, ☎ 216166

Mecsér (H)

Telephone area code: 96

P/Fw Dunaparti, Ady E. u. 45, ☎ 213386

Bh Pusztacsárda 1804, Kisalföldi Lovasközpont Rigópuszta, ☎ 30/5005000

Dunaszeg (H)

Postal code: 9174; Telephone area code: 096

Pz Cseh, Petöfi u. 55, ☎ 352056, I

Pz Vincze Laszloné, Szechenyi u. 8, Dunaszeg, ☎ 602276, I

Pz Horváth, Fö u. 32, I

Pz Molnár, Zrinyi u. 22, ☎ 352156, II

Pz Pércsi, Rákóczi u. 11, ☎ 352137, II

Györ (H)

Postal code: 9021; Telephone area code: 96

🄸 Tourinform Györ, Árpád u. 32, ☎ 311 771

H Alfa, Tihanyi Árpád u. 23, ☎ 316846

H Arany Szarvas Fogadó, Radó sétány 1, ☎ 517452

H Baross, Baross Gábor u. 69, ☎ 516290

H Konferencia, Apor Vilmos püspök tére 3, ☎ 511450, IV

H Golden Ball Club, Szent István u. 4, ☎ 322 360, V

H Klastrom, Zechmeister ut 1, ☎ 516910, III-IV

H Kálvária, Kálvária u. 22D, ☎ 510800

H Paár Szieszta, Attila út 41-43, ☎ 527443

H Pannónia Szálló, Kandó Kálmán u. 1, ☎ 524550

H Rába, Árpád út 34, ☎ 507600, V

H Senator, Bácsai ut 44, ☎ 332336, III

H Schweizerhof, Sarkantyú köz 11-13, ☎ 329171, VI

H Weldi, Pesti út 35-37, ☎ 529540

H Wesselényi, Wesselényi u. 3, ☎ 439620, V

H Fortunátus Szabadidö Klub, Kandó K. u. 15b, ☎ 521688, III

H Szárnyaskerék, Révai u. 5, ☎ 314629, II

P Corvin, Csaba u. 22, ☎ 312171, II

P Csendes Éj, Szabadság u. 52, ☎ 333100

P Fehér Hajó, Kiss Ernö u. 4, ☎ 317608

P Hanekám, Híd u. 12, ☎ 310408

P Hosteria Tia Maria, Eörsy P. u. 17, ☎ 439126

P Hunyadi, Hunyadi u. 10, ☎ 329162

P Kiskút, Kiskúti út 41/A, ☎ 517126

P Pongrácz, Fehérvári út 190, ☎ 410818

P Révész, Hédervári u. 22/b, ☎ 320-667, III

P Sámson, Auróra u. 7, ☎ 419007, III

P Szél Fiai Fogadó, Vaskapu 71, ☎ 540015

P Duna, Vörösmarty u. 5, ☎ 329084, III

P Gróf Cziráky, Bécsi kapu tér 8, ☎ 528466, III

P Hummel, Kálvária u. 57, ☎ 412599, III

P Kertész, Iskola u. 11, ☎ 317461, III

P Kuckó Panzio, Arany János u. 33, ☎ 316260, II

P Petö, Kossuth Lajos u. 20, ☎ 313412, III

P Relax, Rába u. 60, ✆ 315584
P Ringa, Czuczor Gergely u. 12-14, ✆ 310262, III
P Stáció, Kálvária u. 4-10, ✆ 327655, III
P Teátrum, Schweidel u. 7, ✆ 310640, III
🏠 Cirill és Method Alapítvány Vendégháza, Kossuth L. u. 65-67, ✆ 320505
🅰 Napsugár Camping, Külsö Veszprémi u. 19, ✆ 411042

Bábolna (H)

Postal code: 2943; Telephone area code: 34
H Bábolna, József Attila u. 4, ✆ 568450
H Imperial, Mészáros u. 1., ✆ 569284, 569204
Pz Török, Csikótelepi u. 19, ✆ 369317
P Pferdegestüt GmbH, Mészáros u. 1, ✆ 569284
Fw Gémesi, Jégeri út 23, ✆ 369087

Ács (H)

Telephone area code: 34
P Tóth, Fö u. 34, ✆ 386185
🅰 Natura Camping, 1-es számú Föút 1, ✆ 30/9467361

Nagyigmánd (H)

Telephone area code: 34
Pz Horváth, Jókai utca 2, ✆ 356002

Komárom (H)

Postal code: 2900; Telephone area code: 34
🅸 Tourinform, Igmándi út 2, ✆ 540590.

🅸 Komturist-Vértes, Volan Gmbh, ✆ 347390
H Juno, Bem J. u. 5, ✆ 344939, II-V
H Karát, Czuczor Gergely u. 54, ✆ 342222, III-V
H Thermal, Táncsics M. út 38, ✆ 342447, II-III
H Thermalhotel Forrás, Táncsics M. u. 34, ✆ 540177, II
🅱éke, Bajcsy-Zsilinszky u. 8, ✆ 340333, II
H Aqua, Táncsics M. u. 34, ✆ 342190, II-III
H Carrier, Varga József u. 9, ✆ 526445, IV
H Tulipán, Kelemen Laszlo u. 1, ✆ 342604, II
H Komárom Étterme, Harek út 1/b, ✆ 345581
P Kocsis, Táncsics Mihály u. 79, ✆ 342400
P Jonathan, Czuczor Gergely u. 60, ✆ 540740
P Vasmacska, Erzsébet tér 2, ✆ 341342
P Monostor, Batsányi u. 58, ✆ 343000
🏠 Thermál Motel, Táncsics M. u. 38, ✆ 342447, 341222
🅰 Thermal Camping, Táncsics Mihály ú. 38, ✆ 342447, 341222
🅰 Camping Monostor, Batsányi u. 58, ✆ 343000
🅰 Solaris Camping, Táncsics M. u. 34-36, ✆ 342551

Tata (H)

Postal code: 2890; Telephone area code: 34
🅸 Tourinform, Ady Endre u. 9, ✆ 586-046 od.45
H Kristály, Ady Endre út 22, ✆ 383577, III-V

H Öreg-tó, Fáklya u. 1, ✆ 487960, III-V
H Gottwald, Fekete ut 1, ✆ 487927
H Kalóz Fregatt, Almási u. 2, ✆ 382382
H Penta Lux, Boróka u. 10, ✆ 588140
H Casablanca, Ufer von Öreg-tó, ✆ 489586
H Arnold, Tanoda tér 9, ✆ 588028
P Kiss, Bacsó B. u. 54, ✆ 586888
P Monika, Tópart sétány (Öreg tó), ✆ 383208, II
P Parti, Boroka u. 6-8, ✆ 481577, II-III
P Tóvárosi Fogadó, Tópart ut. 11, ✆ 381599
🏠 Öreg-tó Club Hotel, Fáklya út 4, ✆ 487960
🅰 Fényes Fürdö Camping, Fényes fürdö, ✆ 481208
🅰 Öreg-tó Camping, Fáklya út 1, ✆ 383496, 25. April-30. Sept.

Dunaszentmiklós (H)

Postal code: 2897; Telephone area code: 34
H Panorama Residence Duna, Új u. 20, ✆ 591300
P Panorama, road to Neszmely, ✆ 0049/170/8042222
Pz Búzer Károly, Neszemélyi U. 6
Pz Schmidt, Petöfi S. u. 26, ✆ 351-022
Pz Bognárné Varró, Neszmélyi ut. 1/A,, ✆ 491916
Gh Jausenstation, main street, ✆ 0049/171/9122425

Neszmely (H)

Postal code: 2544; Telephone area code: 34
H Hilltop Neszmely Weinhotel, Melegeshegy Pf. 4, ✆ 550440, V
🅰 Eden, Landstraße Nr. 10, ✆ 033/474-183

Süttö (H)

Postal code: 8313; Telephone area code: 33
🅰 Camping „Eden", main street No. 10, ✆ 474327

Labatlan:

H Panorama, Petofi u.5, ✆ 0036/33/462551

Esztergom (H)

Postal code: 2500; Telephone area code: 33
🅸 Gran-Tours, Széchenyi tér 25. ✆ 417052
H Beta Esztergom, Primás-sziget, Nagy-Duna sétány, ✆ 412555, III
H Oktáv, Wesselényi u. 35-39 (Kertváros), ✆ 435755, II-III
P Ria Panzio, Batthyány u. 11-13, ✆ 401428, VI
P Alabardos, Bajcsy-Zsilinszky u. 49, ✆ 312640
P Márta Panzio, Bocskoroskúti út 1, ✆ 311983, II
P Platán, Kis-Duna sétány 11, ✆ 411355
P Decsi, Babits Mihály út 8 ✆ 30-5003350
P St. Georg, Andrássy út. 21, ✆ 502180
P St. Kristóf, Dobozi u. 11, ✆ 414153
P Helemba, Búbánatvölgy, ✆ 313735

P Szalma, Nagy Duna s. 2, ☎ 315336

🏕 Gran Camping, Nagy Duna sétány 3, ☎ 402513

🏕 Golf Ifjúsági, Nagy-Duna sétány 1-3, ☎ 315930

Vác (H)

Postal code: 2600; Telephone area code: 27

ℹ️ Tourinform, Március 15 Tér 16-18, ☎ 316-160

H Grand Hotel, Vegh Dezsö u. 1, ☎ 301864

H Vörössipka, Honvéd u. 14, ☎ 501055

P Naszály Szálló, Sejce Dülő T. ép, ☎ 332649

P Zeke, Zeke u. 5, ☎ 318234

P Csillag Motel, Balassagyarmati út. 8, ☎ 316-421

P Motel 21, Derecske dülö 3, ☎ 317915

P Tabán, Dombay u. 11, ☎ 315-607

P Napsugár, Papp Béla u. 15, ☎ 316490

P Fónagy & Walter, Budapesti főút 36, ☎ 310682

Pz Szabó, Kert u. 3, ☎ 311264, 3823083

Pz Szt. Mihály Apartman, Kápolna u. 8, ☎ 315891, 4567879

Pz Dr. Alt, Tabán u. 28, ☎ 316860

Pz Szivárván, Újhegyi u. 106, ☎ 315831

Szob (H)

Postal code: 2648; Telephone area code: 20

H Zebegényi Kulcsoshász, Külterület, ☎ 346150

P Popeye Fogadó, Zilahy Lajos u. 7, ☎ 3122589, I

Zebegény (H)

Telephone area code: 27

H Kenderes Étterme, Dózsa Gy. u. 26, ☎ ,373444, 370113, II-VI

P Almáskert, Almáskert u. 13, ☎ 373037

Gh Malomkerék, Malom u. 21, ☎ 373010, II

Nagymaros (H)

Postal code: 2626; Telephone area code: 27

H Dunagyöngye Hotel és Étterem, Váci út. 27, ☎ 354045, 594270

Gh Szent István, ☎ 594090, 594091

P Feketesas, Váci u. 27, ☎ 594270

🏚 Törökmezoi turistaház, Törökmező, ☎ 350063

🏕 Camping Nagymaros, Sólyom-sziget, ☎ 594320, 1/4072382

Veröce (H)

Postal code: 2621; Telephone area code: 27

H Fehér Hattyú, ´Árpád u. 60, ☎ 350057, III

Gh Magyarkút, Magyarkúti út 5, ☎ 380587

Pilismarót (H)

Postal code: 2028; Telephone area code: 033

P Alexandra Duna Panzio, Akácos u., ☎ 060 340238 od. 470783

Pz Alischer, Széchenyi u. 18, ☎ 020 431088, I

Pz Benkovics, Dobozi u. 3, ☎ 033 371135

Pz Pergelné, Vár ut. 4, ☎ 033 470260

🏚 Hamvaskö Vadásház, ☎ 033 471169

🏕 Aqua-Camping, danube

Dömös (H)

Postal code: 2027; Telephone area code: 033

Pz Libicz, Felsöfalu u. 33, ☎ 482317, I

🏕 Dömös Camping, Duna-part, ☎ 482319, May - Sept. 15th

Visegrád (H)

Postal code: 2025; Telephone area code: 26

ℹ️ Visegrád Tours, Rév u. 15, ☎ 398160

H Silvanus, Feketehegy, ☎ 398311, VI

H Vár, Fö u. 9, ☎ 397522, V

H Visegrád, Rév u. 15., ☎ 397034, IV

H Danubius Spa, Lepencevölgy, ☎ 801900

Gh Elte, Fö út 117, ☎ 398165

P Villa Tekla, Berkenye u. 12., ☎ 397051

P Honti, Fö u. 66, ☎ 398120, IV-V

Pz Pichler, Fö ut 55, ☎ 398268

Pz Bognár, Rákóczi ut 6, ☎ 398096

Pz Schubauer, Fö u. 135, ☎ 398153

Pz Nádler, Mátyás király u. 9, ☎ 397353

🏕 Kék Duna Autocamping, Fö ut 70, ☎ 398102

🏕 Jurta Camping, Visegrád-Mogyoróhegy, ☎ 398102

Tahitótfalu (H)

Postal code: 2022; Telephone area code: 26

H Tahiti Vendégpark, Dunasor 10, ☎ 385677

P Bernadett, Szabadság tér 4, ☎ 27100, II-III

🏚 Turistaszálló, Semmelweis u. 11, ☎ 27114

🏕 Duna Camping Panzió, Dunasor 10., ☎ 385216

Leányfalu (H)

Postal code: 2016; Telephone area code: 26

H Twins, Moricz Zsigmond 37-39, ☎ 381315

🏕 Camping Donauknie, Leányfalu, Alszeghy tér 1, ☎ 383154 od. ☎ 380764

Szigetmonostor (H)

Postal code: 2015; Telephone area code: 026

H Kék Duna Aktív Üdülöközpont, Duna sor 8, ☎ 393246

Bh Bacchus, Petöfi u. 19, ☎ 393545

Szentendre (H)

Postal code: 2000; Telephone area code: 26

ℹ️ Tourinform, Dumtsa Jenö u. 22, ☎ 317965

H Apolló, Méhész u. 3, ☎ 310909

H Aradi, Aradi u. 4, ☎ 314274

H Átrium, Pátriárka u. 6, ☎ 301800

H Bárczy Fogadó, Bogdányi u. 30, ☎ 310574

H Kentaur, Marx tér 3, ☎ 312125, V

H Danubius, Ady Endre u. 28, ☎ 312489, III-IV

H Duna Club Hotel, Duna korzó 5, ☎ 314102

H Horváth Fogadó, Daru-piac 2, ☎ 313950

H Hubertus, Tyúkos dulo 10, ☎ 310616

H Köhegyi Menedékház, Köhegy 15, ☎ 312292

P Lajosforrási Turistaház, Lajosforrás Pf. 40,
☎ 310683

H Panzió 100, Ady Endre ut 100, ☎ 310661, V

H Bükkös, Bükkös-part 16, ☎ 312021, V

H Provincia, Paprikabíró u. 21-23, ☎ 301082, IV-VI

H Róz, Pannónia u. 6/b, ☎ 311737 , V

P No. 100 Panzió, Ady Endre u. 100, ☎ 310373

P Centrum, Dunakorzó, ☎ 302500, III

P Cola, Dunakanyar krt. 50, ☎ 310410

P Corner, Ady Endre út 28, ☎ 312511

P Ister Luxus, Cseresznyes u. 13, ☎ 312511

P Panorama, Berek u. 32, ☎ 315151

P Villa Castra, Ady E. út 54, ☎ 311240

P Aradi, Aradi u. 4, ☎ 314274

P Ilona, Rákóczi u. 11, ☎ 313599

P Sajti Ház, Csillag köz 5, ☎ 313815

P St. Andrea, Egres út. 22, ☎ 301800, III-IV

P Torony, Iskola u. 1, ☎ 313999

P Zita, Ortorony u. 16, ☎ 313886

🏠 Petöfi Turistaház, Köhegyi út 16, ☎ 312292

🏠 Turistaszálló Márka, Szabadkai u. 9,
☎ 312788

🏕 Aquatours Camping, Ady E. út 9-11,
☎ 311106, 15. April-15. Okt.

🏕 Pap-Sziget Camping, Pap-Sziget, ☎ 310697,
May-Sept.

Budakalász (H)
Postal code: 2011; Telephone area code: 026

P Haus Federer, Lejtö u. 3, ☎ 341802, II

Dobogókö (H)
Postal code: 2099; Telephone area code: 026

H Manreza, Fény u. 1, ☎ 347681

H Pilis, Téry ödön u. 1, ☎ 347522, II-III

H Nimrod, Eötvös Sétány 4-6, ☎ 020/4602134

🏠 Eötvös turistaszálló, ☎ 327644

Pilisszentlászló (H)
Telephone area code: 26

H Pilis, Szentendrei út 8, ☎ 338709

Gh Jánosik, Béke u. 8, ☎ 338093, I-II

P Sissy, Fö u. 157., ☎ 330259

P Gondola, Tü zoltó u. 2, ☎ 331737

Budapest (H)
Telephone area code: 1

ℹ Tourinform, western train station,
☎ 302-8580

ℹ Tourinform, VI. Liszt Ferenc tér 9-11, ☎ 322-4098

ℹ Tourinform, V. Sütö utca 2, ☎ 438-8080.

H Thermal Aquincum Corinthia, Arpád fejedelem útja 94 (Obuda), ☎ 4364100, VI

H Danubius Thermal Margareteninsel, 1138, Margitsziget, ☎ 8894700, VI

H Pannonia Hotel Emke, Blaha Lujza tér/ Akácfa u. 1-3 (City), ☎ 4783050, V

H Orion, Döbrentei u. 13, ☎ 3568583, V-VI

H Parkhotel, Baross tér 10, ☎ 3131422, V

H Lido, Nánási út 67 (Obuda), ☎ 4360980, IV-V

H Liget, Dozsa György ut 106, ☎ 2695300

H Római Hotel, Szent János u. 16 (Obuda),
☎ 3886167, II-III

H Metropol, 1074, Rákóczi út 58 (City), ☎ 4628100, III-V

P Beatrix, Széher út 3 (Buda), ☎ 2750550, IV

P Agi, Jablonka u. 20 (Obuda), ☎ 2503705, III-V

P Büro, Dékán u. 3, ☎ 2122929, III-IV

P Duna Party, Kiralyok u. 93 b, ☎ 2503667, II-III

P Sissi, Kossuth Lajos u. 42 (City), ☎ 2822448, II-III

Pz Dr. Füle Sándorné, Budapest IX, Lónyay u. 25.,
☎ 2179985

🏠 Fortuna Szálloda - és éttermhajó, Szent István park, alsó rakpart (Pest), ☎ 2888100

🏠 Station Guesthouse, Mexikói út 36/B (Pest),
☎ 2218864

🏠 Best Hostel, Podmaniczky u. 27 (Pest),
☎ 3324934

🏠 Hotel Touring, Pünkösdfürdö u. 38 (Buda),
☎ 2503184

🏠 Travellers Hostel Hill, Ménesi út 5 (Buda),
☎ 4132062

🏠 Travellers Hostel Schönherz, Irinyi J. utca 42,
☎ 4132062

🏠 Travellers Hostel Universtias, Irinyi u. 9/11 (Buda), ☎ 4132062

🏠 Travellers Hostel Donáti, Donáti u. 46 (Buda),
☎ 4132062

🏕 Mini-Camping, Királyok útja 307, ☎ 30/9210178

🏕 Camping Római-fürdö, Szentendrei út 189 (Obuda), ☎ 3686260

🏕 Niche Camping, Zugligeti út 101, ☎ 2008346

🏕 Lidó Camping, Üdülösor 2, ☎ 30/9211133

🏕 Csilléberci Camping, Konkoly-Thege u. 21,
☎ 2754033

🏕 Haller Camping, Haller u. 27, ☎ 2166741

Geographical Index

Page numbers printed in *green* refer to the list of accomodations.